The Moral Benefit
of Punishment

The Moral Benefit of Punishment

Self-Determination as a Goal of Correctional Counseling

Frances E. Gill

LEXINGTON BOOKS
Lanham • Boulder • New York • Oxford

LEXINGTON BOOKS

Published in the United States of America
by Lexington Books
A Member of the Rowman & Littlefield Publishing Group
4501 Forbes Boulevard, Suite 200, Lanham, Maryland 20706

PO Box 317
Oxford
OX2 9RU, UK

British Library Cataloguing in Publication Information Available

Library of Congress Cataloging-in-Publication Data

Gill, Frances E., 1953–
    The moral benefit of punishment: self-determination as a goal of
correctional counseling / Frances E. Gill.
        p. cm.
Includes bibliographical references and index.
    ISBN 0-7391-0577-9 (alk. paper)
    1. Criminals—Rehabilitation—Moral and ethical aspects. 2.
Prisoners—Counseling of. 3. Autonomy (Psychology) I. Title.
    HV9276 .G54 2003
365' .66—dc21

2002151170

Printed in the United States of America

♾ ™ The paper used in this publication meets the minimum requirements of
American National Standard for Information Sciences—Permanence of Paper for
Printed Library Materials, ANSI/NISO Z39.48-1992.

Contents

Acknowledgments

In the writing of this book, several of my mentors and friends at the University of Missouri-Columbia were of immense help in providing criticisms and raising questions that improved the work. Robert Johnson, Peter Markie, and Paul Weirich made helpful suggestions during the early research and writing. Richard Thoreson was of great assistance in correcting my schematization of psychological theories in chapter 5. Throughout the entire process of developing this book, John Kultgen's comments and criticisms were of incalculable value.

The crafting of this book was also aided by persons outside of academia. Recollections of past discussions regarding the rehabilitation potential of convicted offenders with Frank Gerner and John Sander, my psychologist associates at Topeka Correctional Facility, helped inspire some of my anecdotal evidence. Finally, the continuing love and support of my family and, most particularly, my husband, Eldon, made the whole project possible.

Introduction

In this work my general aim is to prove that self-determination is a goal of correctional counseling. The idea for this claim originated from an article by Kerry Brace (1992) in which she argues that there are two nonrelativist goals of psychotherapy: respect for persons and self-determination. Brace says that these two ends are present in any instance of psychotherapy or therapeutic counseling. As I regard correctional counseling as a species of therapeutic counseling, it seemed to me to follow that self-determination would also be a goal of the helping professional involved in correctional counseling. This conclusion, however, leads to a puzzle. It could be said that the last thing we want is for convicted felons to be self-determining. We do not want these persons to be freer to act on their criminal desires, for they are already too free in indulging in criminal behavior, and their excessive freedom is the reason we think that the state must restrain them. This sort of freedom, however, is not what correctional counseling is interested in.

My defense of self-determination as a goal of correctional counseling consists of three parts. In the first two chapters I present and argue for a particular conception of the justification of punishment. In the third and fourth chapters I argue for the paternalism of the state that punishes on the basis of a developmental conception of self-determination. In the fifth chapter I show that correctional counselors do in fact try to promote self-determination in their clients. My philosophical proof rests on an analysis of their theoretical commitments. In concluding, I address some important objections and possible implications of the claims I have made.

The view that self-determination is a goal of correctional counseling presupposes a particular account of the justification of punishment, which is the moral education view. Of the various standard alternatives, only this account holds that punishment can be a good or a benefit for the person punished. The moral education account states that punishment can facilitate moral improvements. There seems to be some division as to whether moral education fits within the standard retributivist or deterrence camps, but I think there are important differences between moral education and both sides of the usual debate. Most retributivist theories justify punishment as a good for the person wronged; most deterrence theories justify punishment as a good for society as a whole. Only moral education sees punishment as having some real value to the person punished, and that value as at least part of its justification.

If punishment is entirely an evil to the person punished, then it does not seem likely that correctional counseling could have any aim different from that which counselors provide to the victims of particular horrors such as natural disasters or war. In those situations, counselors merely provide emotional support to help the victims endure a difficult period in their lives. The term "correctional counseling" seems to connote something different. It connotes the idea of correcting to a better way of life, and this idea is a necessary part of the definition I provide for the term in the fifth chapter. If this is correct, it must be that punishment can facilitate positive change, and if punishment can provide this benefit, it makes sense for correctional counseling to be supportive of it.

Consequently, my first project is to show that punishment can facilitate self-improvement, and it is justified when it aims to do so. In the first chapter I present a plausible account of the moral education of punishment. To do so, I commence by briefly exploring the differences between moral education and the standard accounts. I then argue for particular definitions of punishment, just laws for the violations of which we may punish, and rationality. These definitions are important to show how punishment can be either justified or lacking in justification. With these established, I present my own conception of how punishment is justified when it is intended to morally educate. It has much in common with Robert Nozick's "non-teleological retributivism." Subsequently, I argue against the view that the intention to educate morally is sufficient for justified punishing, and I address the specific punishment of incarceration as one justifiable means to the end of moral education.

In the second chapter I present a more extended defense of the necessity of the aim to morally educate those we justifiably punish. First, I examine the weakness of the position of moral nihilists, such as Michel Foucault, who seem to believe that there is no moral justification of punishment. Second, I further examine the distinctions between the standard account of deterrence and moral education. I show that the interest of the just state in punishing is not simply in deterrence, which is an entirely negative goal, but is also in the positive goal of promoting rational, law-abiding behavior. Third, I examine the distinctions between popular standard accounts of retribution and moral education. A notable distinction between moral education and Kantian retributivism is that Kant believes it is impossible to cause other persons to acquire moral ends due to the nature of human freedom. In consideration of this view, Russ Shafer-Landau brings up several apparent difficulties for the moral education account related to the requirement to respect autonomy, and I present an initial answer to his concerns here. Fourth, I explore the distinction between moral education and the self-protection account. While I think the right to self-protection is probably also necessary for the justification of punishment, I argue here that there are several reasons why it is in itself insufficient. I also show that there is no inherent inconsistency between the two accounts, which is important to show that they are mutually necessary. Fifth, I answer several concerns about the practicality of moral education. Sixth and last, I address a specific practical issue, which is whether moral education endorses determinate or indeterminate sentencing. Problems seem to arise for the account with either alternative. I argue that it actually endorses a defensible sentencing policy that is a compromise between determinate and indeterminate.

Punishment that aims to morally educate is paternalistic, and it can also be asked whether the state may act paternalistically in this manner. In the third chapter I present and defend Gerald Dworkin's definition of paternalistic acts and discuss how paternalistic acts in general are justified. I argue that they are justified when two necessary conditions are fulfilled. These conditions are suggested in the work of John Kultgen and Danny Scoccia. They are mindful of the importance of respecting both human and individual needs when we intervene paternalistically and of distinctions in the value of levels of autonomous desires. Next, I argue that the state paternalism of punishment must meet these criteria to be justified, but its sufficient justification requires that it meet some additional standards due to its impersonal nature. These additional standards are provided by Kultgen, and I show that the moral education of state punishment meets these as well. Finally, I argue that this form of state paternalism is a defensible legal moralism and possibly a defensible legal perfectionism as well. In doing so, I address some objections to my view from the liberal camp.

If there are qualitative differences in autonomous desires, then it must be the case that there are different levels of self-determination. I defend this claim in the fourth chapter, where I present a developmental conception of self-determination. Maurice Merleau-Ponty sets the stage for this conception with his view of freedom as an exchange of significations or meanings between the individual and the world he finds himself in. It is more fully explained in the account of Mitchell Aboulafia, who shows how persons progress toward becoming self-determined by means of the internalization of the perspective of the other and the internalization of negation. After presenting Aboulafia's account, I show that the stages by which persons become self-determined parallel Lawrence Kohlberg's stages of moral development. This is important because it shows that progress along the stages of self-determination involve qualitative improvements. That is, as people become increasingly self-determined, their actions and judgments become of increasing value both to themselves and others. In making progress along these stages, their sense of empowerment improves and their vulnerability to the vagaries of chance decreases. Thus, persons who become increasingly self-determined are truly benefited.

In the fifth chapter, I return to the issue of correctional counseling. I start by arguing for a specific definition of correctional counseling, which includes the requirement that the professionals who engage in it have some idea as to the psychological source of criminal behavior in the offenders they work with and how to treat it. Every one of these professionals works from one of four possible general theoretical orientations. These are the psychoanalytic, behaviorist, phenomenological-existential, and rational. Each theory has inspired specific treatment techniques for counselors working with offenders. In this chapter I explore the theories' views of maladaptive behavior and its treatment. In spite of their many differences, I argue that correctional counselors from any of these theoretical orientations are concerned with facilitating progress in self-determination. While there is much variation among the theories in describing the ends of treatment, I show that an important end they each aspire to is consistent with the goal of self-determination that I describe.

In the sixth and final chapter, I address at greater length several remaining objections to my claim. First, I address a worry from Robert Redmon that any claim about the goal of correctional counseling must be normative. I argue that my claim is descriptive because correctional counseling always aims to benefit, though it can fail to do so. A normative conception of correctional counseling would include criteria for success. Second, I examine an objection suggested by Joseph Margolis that the ends of correctional counseling are essentially dictated by social conventions. While I think Margolis correctly points out problems with certain universalist conceptions of mental disorders, I argue that full consideration of human need, and most particularly the human need for a sense of empowerment, can reveal the universality of certain counseling goals. Third, I answer the objection that, even though I show some consistency between the goals of the four psychological theories and my own account of self-determination, these theories are truly consistent with each other. I show that every theory is interested in promoting what I describe as two necessary conditions for self-determination. Finally, I end by briefly discussing some possible philosophical and psychological implications from the claims I have made.

Chapter One

A Presentation of a Moral Education Theory

In this chapter I present a defense of a moral education account of the justification of punishment in order to show that punishment, and specifically incarceration, can be a good for the person punished. To do so, I first clarify what a moral education account is by distinguishing it from the standard accounts of the justification of punishment. I then commence a presentation of a plausible moral education account. In doing so, important concepts within moral education theory are clarified, such as punishment, just laws, just laws for violations of which punishment is permissible, and rationality. Contrasts with other conceptions of moral education theory are discussed, as is the necessity and comprehensibility of this account. The concluding issue is a justification of incarceration as a specific means of punishment, which is an essential issue for a work concerned with explaining why self-determination is a goal of correctional counseling.

DISTINGUISHING MORAL EDUCATION THEORY FROM THE STANDARD JUSTIFICATIONS

The standard accounts for justifying punishment are retributivism and deterrence. The retributivist account generally justifies punishment as a debt owed or deserved by the person punished. Typically, retributivist accounts are regarded as backward-looking in the sense that they only look to the offense as a means of justifying punishment.

The deterrence account, on the other hand, generally justifies punishment as a means of deterring future crime by the wrongdoer or other members of society who contemplate committing the same crime. Typically, deterrence accounts are regarded as forward-looking toward the prevention of future crime.

Whichever justification of punishment is adopted, the justification is based on an advantage or good to some person or persons by means of the punishment. For the standard retributivist, the advantage or good in punishing comes principally from the satisfaction to the victim of having her wrong publicly addressed. For the standard deterrence account, the advantage or good in punishing comes principally from a decrease in future criminal acts against members of society. Neither of these accounts is interested in the advantage or good of the person punished. As such, a common criticism of deterrence is that it can allow the innocent to be punished because there are cases where punishing a scapegoat could deter would-be offenders. Clearly, punishing the innocent scapegoat would be nothing but an evil for him. Retributivism, in its focus on desert, which can be described as an infliction of pain for pain, has been criticized as unduly vindictive.

The moral education view, in contrast to the standard accounts, justifies punishment as a good for the person punished because it claims that punishment is a means toward the moral reform of the person, which can result in the internalization of moral values and a potentially happier life. The moral education view has at times been classified both as a retributivist theory (Nozick) and a deterrence theory (Walker). It has been seen as retributivist because the moral education of a wrongdoer cannot take place unless her punishment is deserved. If it is undeserved, then punishment may only change the person's behavior for the worse because of the justifiable resentment toward the punisher the punishment is likely to cause, which may lead to a sense of alienation from the punisher's standards. On the other hand, moral education theory has been seen as part of deterrence because if someone is morally reformed, then she is likely to be effectively diverted by her new moral motivations from future wrongdoing. Nonetheless, moral education theory is distinct from standard retributivist and deterrence accounts for two reasons.

First, moral education theory is both backward- and forward-looking. It looks back to the act of wrongdoing as one of the reasons for punishing a person. It also looks forward to the future well-being of the person punished, who by means of moral reform is enabled to rejoin the moral community and who thereby can lead a happier and less socially isolated life. The moral education theory presupposes that the wrongdoer acts out of immoral motives to gain her ends even at the cost of injury to other persons or motives to accomplish ends that involve injuring others. A person who is indifferent to others or interested in injuring them will probably be socially isolated and even ostracized. Insofar as humans are essentially social animals who require companionship and affection, the isolated person is hurt by his immoral actions. (It seems probable that both Plato and Herbert Morris, who defend a moral education account, believe that these reasons are sufficient for believing that it is worse to do than to suffer harm.)

Second, and most importantly, only moral education theory maintains that punishment is justified only if it is meant to be a good for the person punished. Only moral education theory finds at least part of the justification in the intrinsic worth of the person upon whom the losses or pain of punishment is being inflicted because the theory fully respects her rationality. However, this concern is conceived in different ways in moral education theory. Some theorists appeal to the troublesome retributivism of Kant or Hegel to claim that punishment respects the intrinsic value of the wrongdoer because she has somehow "willed" her punishment. This is supposed to give her a "right to punishment." This notion is refuted by John Deigh, who points out that it seems very unlikely that anyone has a right to something she would never want except under very strange counterfactual circumstances. However, moral education theory does not have to assert the problematic right of punishment. It can justify punishment by justifying the state acting paternalistically, as I will argue in a later chapter.

Moral education theory, of course, can be challenged at this point with the claim that wrongdoers need not have their advantage considered at all when we punish them. This claim rests on the belief that desert is a sufficient justification for punishment. In answering this objection, most moral education theorists refer to a Platonic view of the state, which is the view that the state is responsible for the moral flourishing of all of its members. These theorists, which include Plato, Hegel, Herbert Morris, Jean Hampton, and R. A. Duff, see the role of the state optimistically as capable of promoting the moral virtue and thereby the happiness of everyone affected by its legal and punitive actions. In doing so, however, these theorists are open to a serious objection from libertarian philosophers who see the state as playing a very limited role in promoting human ends. Libertarians believe that punishment can only be justified when required to protect oneself and others and that the state is incapable of promoting moral ends. I will address this objection in more depth in the next chapter, but I will say at this stage that the objection is not critical for a limited view of moral education. This is because a plausible account of moral education as a necessary condition of the justification of punishment does not require that punishment lead to a complete moral transformation (i.e., an internalization of moral values) but only that it lead to an understanding of the moral limits on actions which the state is imposing by punishing. This sort of change may be considered a partial moral transformation, a transformation only in the recognition of external limits to behavior. My account, however, is not intended to eschew the possibility of a more complete moral transformation, because it would be a great bonus to the person punished as well as for those who punish. I will only show that a complete moral transformation is not necessary for moral education to take place and for the person to be benefited by her punishment.

MY MORAL EDUCATION ACCOUNT
OF THE JUSTIFICATION OF PUNISHMENT

Defining Punishment

To commence my account of moral education, I begin with proposing a workable definition of punishment. Hampton defines punishment as a response to wrongdoing that interferes with a person's freedom to fulfill her desires (129). This definition is consistent with the view of Herbert Morris, who points out that punishment "characteristically involves a deprivation that individuals seek to avoid, with the implication that there is some conflict between what people want and what they get" (45).

The difficulty with Hampton's definition, however, is that it is not sufficiently descriptive of the end that punishment, if it is to be called punishment, is meant to achieve. There are some individuals who do not find punishment in Hampton's terms painful. For instance, some ex-convicts, who are commonly referred to as institutionalized, purposely reoffend in order to be incarcerated because they prefer life inside prison to life in the community. Hampton may argue, of course, that for that class of ex-convicts prison is not a deprivation or a punishment because it is what they desire, yet it seems very doubtful that a loss of liberty is not a deprivation for any rational being. By her definition, the incarceration of the ex-convict who desires incarceration is punishment. Yet that person is probably extremely unlikely to be morally educated by means of his incarceration. In consequence, her definition allows for the possibility that punishment in certain cases can never be justified by a moral education account. In its place, a definition of punishment is needed which would include only those cases that are potentially justified. This implies that only the morally educable or rational can be punished. Animals or irrational persons are merely restrained; they are not punished.

What Hampton's definition lacks is suggested by Duff, who explains in his moral education account that punishment is intended to induce guilt in the person punished. And, if it induces feelings of guilt or moral conflict, then it must be a painful or at least an uncomfortable experience. The idea that punishment, if it is intended to be an agent of change, should be painful or in some sense unpleasant is supported by the experience of psychotherapists. Psychotherapists from varying theoretical backgrounds have observed that for a person to desire to change his habitual behaviors and attitudes, he must realize that these have led to very negative consequences for him in the form of pain or discomfort. A person who finds life generally pleasant will see no need to change himself or his patterns of interacting with others. While he may at times find the satisfaction of his desires for certain ends blocked by barriers constructed by nature or other persons, these barriers in themselves need not be painful. If they are not painful and do not induce in him feelings of frustration at not being able to achieve his goals, then he has little reason to deliberate about constructive strategies to overcome the barriers. Desires are concerned with achieving the pleasant and avoiding the unpleasant. If punishment is intended to instill a desire for moral change, then it surely must be unpleasant for the person punished.

I am suggesting at this point that a workable definition of punishment would be a response to the wrongdoing of a rational person which not only interferes with her freedom to fulfill her desires but which is also intended to induce suffering. Without suffering, the wrongdoer is not likely to find the experience punishing, and he is not likely to develop a desire to end the suffering. Nor is he likely to be concerned with considering means to satisfy his new desire.

Robert Nozick discusses the importance of suffering in punishment if our aim is to facilitate change in the wrongdoer. He says that the wrongdoer flouts correct values and is "anti-linked" or directly opposed to correct values in his acting. As Nozick explains, this anti-linkage is most clearly seen when persons do something wrong simply because it is wrong. One can also be anti-linked (although perhaps to a lesser degree) when acting wrongly in spite of the action's wrongness. It is the job of punishment to have a significant impact on the wrongdoer's life in these cases of anti-linkage in order to reconnect him with correct values. Punishment is meant to make the wrongdoer no longer glad that he acted in opposition to the correct values and to instill in him the desire to no longer flout those values. To get the attention of the wrongdoer, we must, according to Nozick, "hit him over the head" with correct values by having him experience the unpleasant consequences of his "anti-linkage" (Nozick, 374-375; 382-384).

Just Laws

The issue of "correct values" relates to an important criterion for all forms of justified punishment by the moral education account. All of the moral education theories that I have canvassed maintain that punishment is only justified if it is a response to an offense which violates a just law. It cannot be a response to an offense which violates an unjust law because in that event it is unlikely that moral education will result from the punishment. It would be unlikely to connect the person, in Nozick's terms, with correct values because the enforcement of unjust laws is immoral, and one cannot expect moral ends to result from taking immoral means. More simply, by the moral education account, the punisher is a moral teacher. If a moral teacher is not a moral exemplar, then her student will receive a mixed message about what is right and consequently cannot be expected to gain correct moral knowledge. It is thus important to clarify what constitutes a just law for the violation of which punishment is permissible.

Duff makes a distinction between punishment and penalties, which helps to clarify this concept (238-239). There are just laws which require citizens to perform certain actions such as feeding parking meters and paying taxes, but the violations of these laws are not clearly immoral acts. It is to the advantage of the administration of government for such laws to be obeyed. The harm one individual causes to others, however, by not paying taxes or feeding the parking meters may be insubstantial, particularly if governmental agencies have been well funded by other individuals. Insofar as the harm caused by violations of these laws is negligible, it seems doubtful that these acts are immoral. If these violations are not immoral, then punishing the violators with the intention of morally educating them seems pointless. An alternative way of conceiving of an appropriate response to these violations is as penalties. Penalties are not expected to morally educate, and they may be seen as equivalent in moral terms to making restitution. They are also not the same as punishment, here defined, because punishment is intended to induce suffering. When a person accidentally harms another with no intention of inflicting harm, we do not typically punish him (i.e., we do not necessarily intend that he suffer), but we do hold him responsible for his negligence and expect him to pay for the damages caused by his negligence. Violations of such just laws as parking regulations seem to be similarly morally constituted, and the infliction of penalties for not feeding the meter may be seen as a means of making restitution to the state for one's negligence. Thus, violations of just law of this type are not considered appropriate candidates for the criminal courts or for punishment.

Another problem for distinguishing those just laws for the violation of which we may rightfully punish concerns cases of petty theft by individuals who are destitute and who have no other means of surviving. This problem is discussed in more depth by Jeffrie Murphy in "Marxism and Retribution." In any case of theft, the property owner is directly harmed. However, at least in certain capitalistic societies with a large and oppressed lower class, there will be cases of persons who truly have no alternative to stealing if they and their families are to survive. While the upper classes of such societies have an investment in creating and enforcing laws to protect their property, laws to protect property in societies where the wealth and means of survival are so unevenly distributed are most likely unjust. This is because a just law is a law that is not oppressive to persons subject to it. It is not a law that oppresses the many in favor of the few. A just law is a law which persons subject to it can obey without unreasonable harm.

The preceding paragraph does not imply that laws against theft cannot be just or that persons cannot be justly punished for theft, but it limits the application of those laws to persons who are capable of surviving without resorting to theft. I will not address here what survival entails or what constitutes a minimally adequate mode of living. However, if food and shelter sufficient for survival were truly not available to some persons in a society by means of earned income or public or private assistance, then it would not be just for those persons to be punished for stealing. If, on the other hand, an indigent person does have alternatives, then punishment would be just. For a person who need not steal, punishing could help him understand the value the owner places in her property and, if he is amenable to moral improvement, to consider what his feelings would be if his own property were stolen from him. Given that he has alternatives to stealing and that he can be a property owner himself, he should be capable of respecting the feelings and property rights of those others that he harms.

Generally speaking, laws against rape, murder, and assault are uncontroversially just. Violent acts, however, are sometimes rationalized as a necessary means to revolution in countries with oppressive or tyrannical governments. Such acts, however, are generally considered acts of war and subject to different moral constraints than civil acts, and I will not address these here. Violent acts by individuals against individuals, on the other hand, are unproblematically violations of just laws. These violations may be excused, of course, in clear cases of self-defense where the person is in danger of substantial physical harm. Even societies with highly unjust distributions of wealth have just laws against murder, rape, and assault. For even a robber baron, who may in some cases permissibly have his wealth plundered, should not be assaulted. To permit such assaults would be to denigrate the value of human persons. It would be to subject individuals to an unjustifiable harm that would be incapable of benefiting them. Granted, it may be objected that the robber baron would experience psychological harm by losing his prized possessions. However, reflection on his loss may make him consider the fact that he had little right to those possessions. On the other hand, reflection after an assault only informs the victim that the person who assaulted him has little respect for him and for his right not to have unnecessary physical pain inflicted on him. It may also, of course, be objected that assaulting the robber baron would be necessary in order to plunder him, and if a person was starving, that assault could be necessary for survival. This sort of case, however, falls under self-defense, which can excuse the assaulter.

I have included as just those laws for which we may punish—laws against rape, murder, and assault. Laws against theft are also just insofar as they only apply to persons with reasonable alternatives. Duff provides a broader conception of just laws probably due to a Platonic or Hegelian conception of the role of government. He says that the just laws of a community are broken by crimes injurious to that community. The criminal, in Duff's view, acts wrongly both in flouting the duty of care or respect which he owes to his victims as fellow members of the community and in injuring the community itself. The offender injures the community, Duff claims, by injuring its common good by injuring any of its members. One criticism of this conception, which comes from Brenda Baker, is its reliance on the idea of a "common good." While it certainly seems likely that in the case of any community, the cooperation and respect the members of that community have for each other will make social living easier, the benefits occur for individuals and not for the group. Granted that certain small communities working together may have common goals, there are many larger communities, such as nations, where the only common good is the ability of individuals in those communities to achieve their individual goods. Insofar as there is no clear sense of a common good above and beyond the protection of individual goods, Duff's conception of a just law seems unnecessarily complex.

My conception of a just law for violations of which we may punish focuses on the values of individuals rather than the common good. It is the values of individuals that are respected by just laws. Just laws prohibit actions which cause only suffering to those affected by the actions because just laws respect the good of all persons they affect, both victims and offenders. Just laws are thus concerned with the

good and with promoting the good. So, punishment resulting from violations of just laws must in some sense promote the good of those
who are punished.

Rationality

Another necessary criterion for punishment on the moral education
account is that the person punished must be rational. There are two
reasons for not punishing the irrational, which reflect two different
conceptions of irrationality among moral education theorists. Most
say that you cannot punish the irrational because they cannot be
morally educated. The irrational on this account are those who cannot
understand that an offense morally requires punishment, and they will
never be able to comprehend the justice of their punishment. A second
account of irrationality simply entails being unable to consider the
possibility of punishment as a reason not to commit a crime. In the
first account of irrationality, punishment is justified because it aims to
morally transform the wrongdoer. It aims to convince him to accept
(and perhaps even will for himself) his punishment. It aims at promoting the internalization of moral values. The second account settles
for an understanding of the moral limits affected by punishment. Only
if the limits cannot be understood is the person considered on this account to be ineligible for punishment.

The former account of irrationality is expressed by Duff and Morris who, for instance, would classify psychopaths as irrational and
consequently as persons we cannot punish. Duff says that a psychopath who could never understand his punishment as anything
more than a coercive imposition should not be punished (264). Morris says that punishment only applies to those persons who have an
attachment to moral values that was formed early. Consequently,
Morris omits the psychopath from consideration for punishment.
Perhaps he considers rationality equivalent to having some minimal
moral standards. Morris suggests that one must be at least minimally
moral (have made a "general" commitment to the basic values underlying the just legal norms that apply to them) to be amenable to
the moral education that punishment can provide (52). By urging us
to not punish the psychopath, Duff and Morris leave us with the
question of what we should do with those individuals. It seems that

they leave us with no choice but to cage the true psychopath like a wild animal. We do not punish animals. Rather, we restrain them by caging, and we condition them. It seems that Duff and Morris would thus have us treat the psychopath as less than human.

Duff and Hampton respond to this concern by following Hegel's lead. Hegel claims that we should not give up on anyone where there is the remotest chance of a flicker of moral improvement, for to give up is to treat the person as less than rational, as no more than an animal. Duff suggests, perhaps in response to the possible objection that such treatment would be demeaning, that we should be extremely cautious and reluctant in labeling anyone as a true psychopath. Hampton goes further and suggests that we should never give up on anyone, even those whom we have reason to believe are incapable of moral change.

The position of Morris, Duff, and Hampton is problematic because there are many individuals in our prison systems (though they remain a minority) who appear to be correctly diagnosed as having an "antisocial personality disorder" (DSM-IV), the current American Psychiatric Association term for psychopathy. While those diagnoses are never certain since they are derived from psychological testing and the judgment of clinical interviewers, in many cases they are very likely correct. It does not seem appropriate to either release or cage these individuals. To release them would be contrary to concern for the safety of the public at large and would express a lack of regard for the seriousness of the offense to the victim. To cage these individuals, on the other hand, would be to ignore the minimal rationality that they do have, for most psychopaths can still be regarded as rational by the second account. By the second account, you are rational as long as you can be motivated by prudential reasons. While psychopaths are very impulsive individuals, they can come in time to understand that certain behaviors have certain consequences and that society frowns on their criminal offenses even though they themselves do not see their offenses negatively.

Roger Greene's description of persons who receive high scores on the Psychopathic Deviate scale of the Minnesota Multiphasic Personality Inventory (MMPI) provides evidence for this last point (86-89). High scorers, according to Greene, are likely to be angry, impulsive, emotionally shallow, unreliable, egocentric, irresponsible, and rebellious. He says they are socially nonconforming, disregarding social rules and conventions in general and authority figures in particular. Further, Greene says they have a long history of inadequate familial and social relationships, which seems to reflect a characterological adjustment. Greene says that they may be unable to learn from experience or to plan ahead and that psychological intervention is usually less effective than maturation in achieving change with these persons. Greene's research suggests that since older adults are usually less impulsive than adolescents, who are much quicker to act on their desires before full reflection on the consequences of acting on those desires takes place, the older psychopath is more capable of reflecting on the consequences of his actions. Consequently, if the psychopath can at some time in his life reflect on the adverse consequences of his actions, he is not wholly lacking in rationality, even though it cannot be anticipated that he will ever be capable of internalizing moral values or in any way empathizing with the needs and concerns of others.

A capacity to understand and act in view of the consequences to oneself of various actions can be described as prudential rationality. It is a capacity which the psychopath seems to have, though he may not act on it until he is of a more advanced age. It is clearly a capacity which animals lack. While animals may be controlled by such things as electrified fences, those fences are never a reason for them to stay within a certain area. Animal response to such control is unthinking and merely conditioned. Setting limits such as prison walls to human wrongdoers is not mere conditioning. Prison walls and animal fences both limit freedom of movement, but only the walls constitute reasons or consequences for certain behaviors that prisoners can consider in their acting. Being reasons or consequences, they appeal to the understanding of the person punished.

Thus, the post-Hegel moral education theorists who seem to believe that only those capable of internalizing moral values and of accepting punishment as just are rational are mistaken. Psychopaths, for example, appear to have some capacity for being prudentially rational though they lack the capacity for complete moral reform.

There are other advantages to the second account of irrationality. While some like Morris say that we may not punish the ignorant or those who have no notion of the immorality of their offense, the second account allows punishers to say that the wrongdoer, being at least minimally rational, should have known better. For instance, it is conceivable that a person who has tortured small children could say in his defense that he was ignorant of the moral law and that no one had ever told him that such behavior is not permissible. However, it is not conceivable that anyone would not believe that this person should have known better, unless he is clearly so insane as to be incapable of understanding that his actions have certain consequences.

Another problem for the first account of rationality is discussed by Nozick, who says that we would want to punish Hitler even though we are fully confident we could never fully reform him. Some acts, Nozick claims, "are so monstrous that a criterion of the agent's understanding their nature is that his realization itself involves (and leads to) a suffering comparable to what matching punishment would inflict" (373). It would be inconceivable to construct a punishment sufficiently averse to fully morally educate Hitler, according to Nozick, because a full understanding of the consequences of his actions through attaining complete empathy with his victims would probably result in excruciating horror and self-destruction. Since he could not survive such knowledge, the requirement of morally educating him in a complete sense could not be met. Yet, we certainly do not want to not punish Hitler; nor do we want to treat him like an animal, which is not in any sense morally responsible for its actions.

A possibly related objection to moral education pertains to punishment which involves incarceration with no possibility for parole. This is related to the Hitler case only in the sense that society generally regards persons given these types of sentences as having little or no potential for reform. By the second account, we intend that punishment at least appeal to the person's prudential rationality. It can be objected that any form of moral education is pointless if the person will never be released. That objection, however, ignores the fact that some incarcerated persons exist for many years within a small, confined penal society. It should be in the interest of the person punished as well as the interest of his fellow inmates and correctional staff for him to recognize the need to modify his behavior toward others for however long he continues to live.

Finally, all moral education theorists demand that the autonomy of the person punished be respected. Thus, they claim that the wrongdoer has the right to refuse to learn the lessons of punishment and to internalize moral values. But, if he has the right to refuse this, then it appears that the punishment is not justified should he in fact refuse. Moral education theorists, such as Duff, however, respond that punishment is justified if complete moral reform is merely attempted or aimed at by the punisher. The difficulty for Duff, however, is that we know there are certain persons, such as the undiagnosed psychopaths, whom we can try to reform completely, and we will never succeed. The intention in these cases seems pointless and insufficient to justify the punishment.

For those moral education theorists who are satisfied with a partial moral reform or an understanding of the moral limits as an aim of punishment, there is no problem with refusal. Should the wrongdoer refuse to internalize moral values and should he maintain that the reason he is punished is based on conventional standards that he does not choose for himself, we are still allowed to punish him. The justifiably punished wrongdoer is able to understand that other people object to his behavior for reasons of their own. He can understand that they have reasons for punishing him even if he does not accept or agree with their reasons. In understanding their reasons for punishing him, he can choose to modify his behavior for purely prudential reasons. He has the right to refuse to modify his behaviors, but he should be able to understand through punishment the consequences of that refusal. Of course, he may also decline to understand the message of punishment, perhaps out of sheer stubbornness, but as long as he has the capacity to understand, he can be punished.

A Nozickian View of Moral Education

The moral education account of the justification of punishment which I am endorsing is much like Nozick's "non-teleological retributivism" (non-TR). Interestingly, Nozick does not refer to his retributivist account as moral education, although other philosophers have described it as such (e.g., Shafer-Landau). Nozick says that the teleological retributivist account (TR) justifies punishment as right due to the consequences (moral reform) to which it might lead. TR is based on an optimistic hypothesis about what another person will become or can come to know. Nozick says that his non-TR account is less optimistic, and it sees punishment as right or good in itself, apart from the further consequences to which it might lead. However, in Nozick's view the act of punishment as an act of retributive justice is meant to connect the wrongdoer to correct values. He says that in doing wrong the person has become disconnected from them (374). Thus, there is a consequence that Nozick thinks punishment should fulfill. It is at least the connection with correct values. There is further evidence that Nozick is presenting a moral education account.

Nozick argues that there are three ways in which correct values can affect our lives: 1) we can do acts because they are right or good; 2) having acted wrongly, we can repent, and give this repentance effect in our lives by, for example, performing repentant actions; and 3) we can have the connection imposed upon us via punishment (374). While Nozick acknowledges that repentance or remorse is a superior means of reconnecting to correct values than the third option, he argues that the imposition of the connection via punishment is sufficient to justify it. The only difficulty for Nozick in making this claim, however, is that he does not really mean that the imposition of punishment is sufficient. Nozick later states that by means of punishment, the wrongdoer's link with incorrect values is wiped out or at least attenuated, "so that he now *regrets* having followed them or at least is less pleased that he did" (379) (emphasis added). So, Nozick wants regret from the wrongdoer, and punishment seems to be an effective means of obtaining that regret. Insofar as regret is a sought after consequence of punishment and a necessary goal of the punisher, who Nozick also says must cause the wrongdoer to suffer, it seems that Nozick also finds the justification for punishment in one of its consequences. He is simply demanding less of punishment than the moral education theorists who insist that remorse is a necessary goal.

Many moral education theorists argue that punishment has an expressive function. It communicates to others that the wrong committed was in fact wrong. It communicates to the wrongdoer that he was at fault; it communicates to the public that such behavior should not and will not be tolerated in silence; and it communicates to the victim that his rights are worth respecting and enforcing. In Nozickian terms, this communication serves to link the wrongdoer with correct values in three ways: 1) punishment insures that the correct values have an effect either in the wrongdoer or on him; 2) it insures that those who punish remain linked with correct values, for in failing to punish, the punishers would become disconnected with the correct values; and 3) it insures a connection with correct values in the relation between the punisher and the wrongdoer. This is a rightness not completely reducible to the effect of punishment on either party but rather has to do with, as Nozick describes, a sort of contractual sense of obligation between them. I believe what he means is that each party is obligated to uphold correct values by participating in the inflicting or the suffering of punishment (379).

As Nozick suggests, it is the linkage or relinkage with correct values that is the benefit and point of punishment, and it is a creation of harmony from the disharmony affected by anti-linkage. While Nozick does not attempt to show how this linkage can be a benefit to the person punished, I think punishment, even if it only has an effect *on* the wrongdoer and not *in* him, can be regarded as a benefit to that person. For even if the wrongdoer does not accept that his punishment is justified and does not begin to internalize moral values as a consequence of it, he is benefited if he at least begins to regret his act of wrongdoing. He is benefited because he now understands the consequences of taking immoral means. He now sees the value of taking only moral means to whatever ends he desires, for he sees moral means as of value for prudential reasons. Moral means will not result in punishment, and he has a better chance of reaching his goals by acting on the prudential reason not to take immoral means.

It is granted that the wrongdoer who does not internalize moral values should not be regarded as a full-fledged member of the moral community and is not a full-fledged member of the kingdom of ends in a Kantian sense. Most moral education theorists think the wrongdoer is benefited by punishment only if punishment helps him to internalize moral values because they accept the Platonic view that *eudaimonia* requires moral virtue. It can be argued, however, that Plato never fully satisfactorily answered Glaucon's challenge. If the end of punishment is to convince wrongdoers to take moral means and if punishment is successful in this goal, then others will perceive the wrongdoer acting rightly in his future dealings with them. Others may not be aware that the former wrongdoer has little regard for truly moral ends and is merely being practical, but they may well be satisfied with the change in his behavior. Hence, it is quite likely that he will be capable of resuming adequate (though perhaps not ideal, in an Aristotelian sense) relationships with others. On the other hand, if he had not come to regret his punishment and the suffering it imposed on him, he would have experienced little motivation for eschewing those means sure to alienate him from others. Social alienation is an evil for any person. If punishment can communicate the necessity of taking moral means (means not involving the abuse or exploitation of others), then it will make possible the renewal of minimally adequate social relations and thus will surely be a good to the person punished.

Necessary But Not Sufficient

I have not argued in this chapter that moral education is sufficient to justify punishment. I have tried to show that it is necessary because punishers should not be indifferent to the good of the persons they cause to suffer. However, I do not believe that moral education is sufficient to justify punishment because justification also requires consideration of the good of others who are affected by an offense. Moral education accounts are mistakenly concerned exclusively with the good of the punished person and neglect the goods of the victim and society.

Hampton alone claims that moral education is sufficient to justify punishment. She acknowledges that punishment benefits the victim by having her wrong publicly addressed and that punishment benefits society by educating all potential perpetrators of the likely consequences of certain acts. However, what is critical according to her account is not the benefit to the victim or to society but the benefit to the person punished. If and only if the person punished is benefited is the punishment justified. Should a person be morally educated by means of a secret punishment that is unknown to the victim or society, then it would be successful on Hampton's account.

Morris, for one, takes this worry into account when he says that moral education is only necessary but not sufficient to justify punishment. He suggests that deterrence or retribution should supplement moral education, though he is inclined to give moral education more weight.

It is very likely that an account such as the one given by Warren Quinn, which justifies punishment as a means for persons to protect themselves against wrongful acts, would also form part of a comprehensive theory. Quinn's account is mindful of the rights of persons to use appropriate means to defend themselves and their property, and as he claims, of the fact that sometimes only the risk of real punishment will be an effective means of self-protection. I am inclined to believe that a moral education account coupled with a self-protection account may provide a sufficient basis for justifying punishment. I will pursue this argument of the necessity of moral education in conjunction with self-protection further in the next chapter.

Incarceration as a Means of Punishing

To say that punishment is justified as a means of morally educating wrongdoers is not to say that every means of punishment is justified. However, there are grounds for believing that incarceration in certain cases is required to meet the goal of moral education. Some alternatives in this country include fines, probationary supervision, and in some select cases capital punishment. I do not intend to address the justification of capital punishment in this work because my concern is with correctional counseling, counseling with the typical aim of preparing inmates for eventual release and reentry into society. Historic alternatives, such as banishment and torture, are no longer considered acceptable means of punishing wrongdoers. Of the two alternatives remaining, fines and probationary supervision are lighter forms of punishing. Incarceration can be described as hard treatment.

Duff provides a good argument in defense of hard treatment for the wrongdoer. Duff claims that only by this means will we *effectively* communicate our condemnation to the criminal. He contrasts hard treatment with merely symbolic punishments in which, for example, the offender is convicted (and thus condemned) and then released, or in which the only suffering caused to the offender is on account of the public condemnation of his offense (i.e., the public humiliation). Duff faults such symbolic punishments for failing to adequately express the appropriate response to wrongdoing (or ineffectual linkage in Nozickian terms). Duff states, however, that some may argue that what this claim reveals is that the expressive function of punishment must be tied in to a consequentialist (deterrent) account or a retributivist (desert) account. Alternatively, if the primary purpose of punishment is expressive, its goal would appear to be eliciting a recognition of guilt and remorse in the offender, and Duff acknowledges, a purely symbolic system could satisfy that purpose. Hence, it is not actually the expressive function of punishment that hard treatment such as imprisonment is meant to fulfill. What it does, Duff claims, is it "translates the disesteem of society into the value system of the recalcitrant individual" (244). For Duff, punishment is a forcible exercise in universalizing an attempt to bring home to the offender the injury he has done to others, in fact rather than merely in imagination, by imposing on him what he will perceive as injurious to himself (240-245).

It is essential that punishment be injurious so that it will at least elicit regret in the wrongdoer. Preferably it will elicit remorse in him. By means of regret or remorse, the goal of moral education is accomplished, which as I have argued, is essential for the punishment to benefit the wrongdoer. Merely fining an individual who has committed murder or rape or placing him on probation is a slap on the wrist, which can easily be shrugged off by the perpetrator. In some cases it can be imagined that a person who assaults an enemy will quite gleefully pay the fine for the pleasure he has received in committing the assault. Certainly, fines and probationary supervision for serious violent offenses fail to communicate the degree of censure society places on such offenses. More importantly, they are not likely to elicit the sort of reaction in the offender which is necessary for moral education to take place.

Duff correctly claims that there probably is no objective standard for the types and lengths of sentences for specific offenses (280). It does not seem correct to say that a two-year prison sentence is an objectively correct punishment for a case of aggravated assault or that a minimum of five years in prison is the objectively correct punishment for a case of rape. Rather, these sentences seem just to us (assuming they do) because of conventional standards. These are the sorts of punishments most people would expect to receive in our society, and most would regard them as justly meted out. On the basis of conventional standards, they seem to be proportionate to the offense. Their proportionality seems correct, however, only because they seem to be adequate lengths of incarceration for the moral message to be communicated and for the wrongdoer to hear and appropriately react to the message through regret or remorse. So, we can say that there are correct conventional standards relative to public perceptions of justly proportionate punishments. In our society, incarceration meets this standard of a justly proportionate punishment for many offenses.

There remains an objection to incarceration and other forms of punishment as means to morally educate persons. It is that if moral education can be accomplished by other, less painful means, we have no need to punish. Nozick provides the example of cases of spiritual transformation in which persons of bad moral character are thereby connected with correct values (i.e., morally as well as spiritually transformed). Nozick relates how the lives of glowing and inspiring sages such as the Buddha, Aurobindo, and the Baal Shem Tov affected and transformed their followers' lives. Granted, there is a practical difficulty with this alternative in that such sages are difficult to come by if one wants wrongdoers to submit to their positive influences. Regardless, Nozick argues that even if the Buddha were more accessible and available to our current crop of wrongdoers, moral education via spiritual transformation would be an inadequate response to certain types of wrongdoing. Nozick doubts that we would be satisfied with the spiritual transformation of Hitler if in the process of being morally educated Hitler experienced no pain or injury to himself. While Nozick admits that vindictive feelings could be the source of our desire for Hitler to suffer, he provides two more defensible reasons for this desire. First, only by the infliction of suffering on great evildoers, Nozick claims, can we be certain that they in no way remain glad that they performed the offense. Second, only the infliction of great suffering is an adequate response to a terrible offense as "wrong qua wrong." Connection to correct values requires that rightness be responded to as right and that wrongness be responded to as wrong, and to ignore the wrongness of the act is to ignore a "significant portion of moral reality" (384-388).

The preceding argument certainly reveals Nozick's strong retributivist orientation because the issue of desert is strongly implied in the justification of punishment as a response to a wrong qua wrong. However, the issue of desert can be regarded as having secondary importance within a theory that holds moral education to be of primary importance while also eschewing the use of spiritually transformative experiences as substitutes for punishment in morally educating wrongdoers. The problem with spiritual transformation is that it does not clearly communicate to the offender his moral responsibility for his act of wrongdoing. It does not require him to suffer and so does not pave the way for reflection on the wrongness of his offense. It does not directly communicate that he must use only moral means in the future or risk future punishments. Finally, it disregards the concern of the victim and the society that the offense be responded to adequately and proportionately. It is a response to a wrong qua wrong but not in the sense of an eye for an eye. Rather, it essentially teaches the wrongdoer he was responsible for his offense, and he must learn to be more responsible in the future or take the consequences.

Chapter Two

A Defense of the Need
for a Moral Education Account

Philosophical criticism of the moral education account of the justification of punishment has included a wide array of objections. In this chapter I defend the necessity of moral education against these objections by arguing that there is some moral justification for punishment, no alternative to moral education is sufficient to justify punishment, moral education does not collapse into any alternative account, and moral education is a practical or feasible goal of punishing. Of the alternative accounts, I think it is very likely that self-protection is also a necessary part of the justification of punishment. If both are necessary, however, problems with determining justification arise if these two purposes can conflict. Hence, I also show that the self-protection and moral education accounts are compatible.

In considering alternative accounts, I do not intend to address every reason that philosophers have considered in justifying punishment. However, as I indicated previously, these reasons have generally fallen into two camps—deterrence and retributivism. Deterrence has had strong advocates, and even some well-known retributivists such as Kant and Rawls have held that legislators should be concerned with the deterrent effects when determining appropriate punishments for different types of crime. Deterrence theories in general justify punishment for the purpose of reducing crime, whether among the general population or by the particular offender who is being punished. Retributivist theories, on the other hand, claim that the punishment of any individual is justified as a response to a wrongful action performed by that person even if it is not a deterrent of further actions. Retributivists, such as Kant and Rawls, think that any specific judicial punishment meted out to individuals must meet this standard. Rawls in particular distinguishes legislative and judicial goals in determining appropriate punishment (i.e., punishment as a societal practice versus punishment as a response to a particular offense) because legislators are rightly concerned with furthering the interests of society while judges are rightly concerned with guilt. Self-protection is a third account that has been widely advocated by Libertarian philosophers. Quinn has argued that it falls under neither of the standard accounts. This account holds that we have the right to threaten to punish as a means to protect ourselves from persons who would violate our rights, and we can actually punish because the threat will not serve to protect us if it is not real. I will examine all three of these accounts in relation to moral education, for I believe that these accounts comprise the list of eligible alternatives.

PUNISHMENT CAN BE MORALLY JUSTIFIED

Few philosophers have taken the extreme position that punishment is never morally justified. This position seems counterintuitive, and it is opposed to the common belief in the human rights to life and liberty. If persons have these rights, then they must have the right to protect and preserve them, which in some cases can require the punishment of those who would infringe them. One philosopher who takes the extreme position is Michel Foucault, who may be regarded as a moral nihilist.

In *Discipline and Punish*, Foucault compares the classical and modern methods of prosecuting and punishing crimes. He relates that in the classical era (before the late eighteenth century) there was no presumption of innocence until guilt was proven. Even a mild degree of suspicion was taken to indicate a mild degree of guilt. Punishment was directed at and inflicted upon the body of the offender by means of public torture and execution because the body was the living representation of the offense. In the modern era where innocence is presumed, punishment is directed at the character of the offender (and not the body). It is striking that Foucault sees nothing intrinsically good about the modern belief in the presumption of innocence and the prohibition against cruel and unusual punishment. Rather, he thinks that the classical and modern practices are simply the most efficacious means of controlling illegalities by persons in power at particular times in history. He speaks of "power relations" between those in power in a society and those under their control. His view of the value of the different power relations of the classical or modern eras is clear when he says

> We must cease once and for all to describe the effects of power in negative terms: it "excludes," it "represses," it "censors," it "abstracts," it "masks," it "conceals." In fact, power produces; it produces reality, it produces domains of objects and rituals of truth. The individual and the knowledge that may be gained of him belong to this production (Foucault, 194).

For Foucault, therefore, the prevailing power relations produce truth, reality, and value. Punishment is not *morally* justified in any era. Rather, he believes the purpose of punishment is only accomplished if it succeeds in effectively maintaining the status quo or in keeping the state whole by preventing revolution and anarchy.

The difficulty with Foucault's view of punishment is inherent in any nihilist position. Nihilists must be careful to avoid finding moral value in *anything* lest they contradict themselves. I think it is of some interest that Foucault at least implicitly finds value in the bohemian life or the free spirit in his book. He gleefully describes the case of a carefree, unemployed vagrant whose lifestyle was at odds with the state's desire to keep those under its domain classified and monitored. It is my impression that Foucault values freedom and individual resistance to state control in spite of his disclaimer. Consequently, if freedom is of value for Foucault (as it seems to be), it must be worth preserving. Insofar as the preservation of freedom requires us to take action against those who would interfere with it and insofar as that action must be punishment, Foucault must, therefore, acknowledge that some form of punishment is morally justifiable.

Of course, it may be objected that Foucault only endorses individual resistance to the infringement of freedom. If only individuals are morally justified in punishing, it does not follow that the state is morally justified. The moral justification of punishment by the state

probably presupposes some contractarian basis for individuals to relinquish their individual rights to punish to the state, which Foucault
may not accept. I will not fully argue here the complicated issue of the
state's right to punish as based on individual rights to punish. However, insofar as many individuals who have the right and the need to
protect themselves have no ability to punish without the aid of the
state, there is reason to believe that the moral justification for punishment by individuals is transferable to the state.

DETERRENCE

The insufficiency of deterrence as a justification for punishment
has been well argued elsewhere, especially by Duff. If the punishment of a specific offense is an effective deterrent, it prevents or reduces the amount of like offenses occurring in the future in a particular society. Other would-be perpetrators of a like offense are
discouraged by learning of the punishment, or at least the person
who is punished finds the punishment sufficiently aversive to modify her future behavior. Deterrence is held to be insufficient chiefly
because its focus is entirely on future outcomes, and actual guilt is
of secondary importance. The guilt of the person punished is of
concern from a deterrence standpoint only indirectly because it
seems likely that a state that frequently punished the innocent
would be less successful in deterring crime. However, it is conceivable that occasional punishment of the innocent when they are
presumed guilty by the general public may be an effective deterrent
to would-be perpetrators. Given this possibility, individual rights
are at risk by punishment for deterrence, which constitutes a significant problem for this justification.

I have previously argued that guilt is essential in the moral education account because moral education cannot occur unless the person
actually commits the offense for which she is punished. Thus, guilt is
of primary importance for moral education. There is another reason,
moreover, to believe that moral education is distinct from deterrence.
It is that moral education theory provides a positive account of what
the state is trying to accomplish in punishing while deterrence theory
only provides a negative account.

It has been objected that moral education, when defensible, collapses into deterrence. Michael Clark argues that since moral education via punishment is a paternalistic and expensive means of morally educating wrongdoers, moral education theorists cannot explain why the state should care to be involved with such means unless it can be proven that moral reform is an effective means of deterrence. Shafer-Landau also doubts that the state has any interest in the moral education of offenders unless it deters. He claims that the moral education of prisoners most often requires expensive rehabilitative programs in addition to incarceration, which the state has difficulty justifying either when innocent persons are in need or when they are not.

Implicit in the deterrence views of Clark and Shafer-Landau is a view of the state as an impersonal arbiter or settler of conflicts between individual members of the state. The state resolves such conflicts only by conferring benefits to the worthy (or innocent) and punishments or penalties to those deemed unworthy (or guilty). They do not consider, however, that in enforcing laws, the state is communicating that it values and commends innocent or law-abiding behavior and devalues and deplores guilty or law-breaking behavior. It rewards the law-abiding members of the state by protecting them with laws that punish those who mean to take advantage of them.

It can be argued that if innocence is truly a value to the state, as the objectors admit, then the state is concerned with promoting innocence in the future in criminal offenders. The state can promote innocence by encouraging wrongdoers to acquire the sort of moral character that will be law-abiding and innocent. Shafer-Landau is correct that punishment without rehabilitative programs will often be insufficient for moral education. In many cases, the moral education of offenders will require both punishment and rehabilitative programs. Rehabilitative programs can include psychotherapy, Alcoholics Anonymous (AA) or Narcotics Anonymous (NA) meetings, substance abuse treatment, secondary and post-secondary education, and vocational education. These programs are often offered in prisons and are sometimes required as part of probationary and parole plans. While Shafer-Landau is correct about the frequent insufficiency of punishment, he does not consider that punishment alone can elicit regret in an offender and thereby begin the process of positive change. In some persons, the experience of regret may be sufficient. Furthermore, in cases of persons for whom punishment alone is not sufficient, the state does have an interest in providing rehabilitative programs because it is concerned about making it possible for all persons subject to its laws to be able to obey them. The state has this concern insofar as its laws are just and the state means to promote rational behavior and to discourage irrational behavior.

I have previously claimed that just laws promote the good for all persons subject to those laws. This is a justifiable paternalism for persons who do not endorse these laws because the enforcement of just laws meant to protect persons and necessary social institutions from harm entails promoting actions based on rational desire and discouraging actions based on irrational desire, specifically the irrational desire to take immoral means. Rationality is a good for agents that all states with just laws actually promote. A concern for rationality is also essential in the enforcement of just laws because persons can only justifiably be punished if they are capable of following the laws. That is, persons who may be punished must have some capacity for prudential rationality, and they must have real alternatives to committing offenses. Rationality, therefore, is of great concern to the state that legitimately punishes.

In the moral education view, punishment is meant to promote the process of change by eliciting remorse in an offender. Punishment functions to help the offender experience a crisis of character. As Richard Prust has argued, in punishing we mean to frustrate some of the offender's desires by having her face the consequences of maintaining a character that leads her to act criminally. The loss of freedom eliminates the possibility of her fulfilling some of her goals. Thus, punishment is meant to precipitate a disruption in the equilibrium of her intentional life so that she will desire to become a person who will no longer commit criminal offenses. For certain persons, the change can only be made permanent by a rehabilitative program. Persons who are deficient in social, academic, and/or vocational skills may lack the ability to maintain their new character over time even with the desire for change. Persons whose psychological difficulties contributed to their offenses may also be unable to make permanent character changes in spite of having the desire to do so.

Take the case of a young man who has been convicted of dealing drugs and who has always lived in an urban ghetto. Suppose he has little formal schooling and no vocational skills, and he is addicted to drugs. If the young man has had no opportunity while in prison to receive high school general equivalency degree (GED) classes, vocational training, or drug treatment (perhaps NA meetings), then he will probably find it impossible to refrain from drug dealing when he returns to his home community. The experience of incarceration alone may have been quite unpleasant and provided an adequate impetus to the reform process, but lacking the skills requisite for success in the community, permanent reform will be a practical impossibility. It is, of course, possible that a rehabilitative program would not be adequate to sustain permanent moral change, but the probability of permanent moral change is much greater with such a program than without it.

There are many cases of offenders whose psychological disorders contributed to violent assaults on others. These disorders can often be treated by psychotherapy, which can eradicate or at least lessen the probability of future violent assaults. These are persons who are not regarded as sufficiently mentally ill (or sufficiently irrational) to qualify for placement in state mental hospitals. The state surely has an interest in promoting rational self-control among these persons by means of psychotherapy.

Rehabilitative programs that further moral education need not be expensive. NA and AA are volunteer organizations. Academic tutoring can be provided by volunteers. American prisons find it generally cost effective to have psychologists on staff if for no other reason than to protect prison staff against violent outbursts by inmates. Poor countries that claim they cannot afford any of these types of programs for either their prisoners or their general population may not respect the rationality of either prisoners or citizens. If the citizens lack the skills requisite to obey the laws, they will not be able to maintain their innocence for long, and the threat of prison will not be a sufficient reason for them not to offend. A prison term in these countries would not be punishment but only a period of being caged or of being treated as a nonrational animal.

One virtue of moral education theory is that it is very compassionate. It is based on genuine concern for the well-being of all persons, and particularly persons whom we affect in our acts of punishing. Moral education theory endorses societies that act out of genuine regard for all persons, not only the innocent but the potentially innocent as well. Offenders can be regarded as having some value by virtue of their potentiality for at least prudential rationality and possibly more, and consequently deserving of benefits conferred by the state.

The preceding argument shows that moral education differs importantly from deterrence because it views punishment positively while deterrence views punishment negatively. Deterrence aims only at eliminating harmful behavior and not at promoting beneficial behavior. It is focused only on a negative end in seeking to control behavior. Moral education, on the other hand, promotes the good of behaving rationally or of taking only moral means to one's ends and is consequently focused on the positive end of human well-being. Moral education also differs from deterrence in that it only justifies punishment of the guilty, which some believe makes it a form of retributivism.

RETRIBUTIVISM

Defined most broadly, the retributivist account of the justification of punishment says that punishment is justified by an offense that a person actually and culpably committed. By this justification, punishment is *deserved* for a wrong performed. It is the sense of retribution that Nozick intends when he describes moral education theory as a teleological retributivism because this account conceives desert as necessary. The standard retributivist account, endorsed by philosophers such as Kant, holds that desert is a sufficient as well as a necessary justification for punishment. The moral education account, however, does not construe desert alone as sufficient. Rather, moral education as a justification for punishment necessarily includes the intention to morally reform the offender. Thus, moral education is distinct from Kantian retributivism, but it may be regarded as one form of general retributivist theory, given the correctness of the broad definition, because moral education accepts desert as necessary.

Kant would be clearly opposed to the traditional moral education accounts of Hampton, Morris, and Duff. Kant believes that it is impossible to make someone adopt a moral end because they must be freely chosen. For Kant, respecting persons entails respecting their choices, however bad they may be. Kant, however, would not be opposed to my moral education account. In my account, moral education takes place when the person punished recognizes the need to take moral means. She need not adopt moral ends to be morally educated. Hence, there is no question that her moral autonomy is not being violated because she remains free to choose her own ends.

In contrast with Kant, I have said that punishment can influence some persons to adopt moral ends even though this is not necessary for punishment to be successful. Like Kant, however, I believe that whenever we punish, the moral autonomy of the person we punish must be respected.

Shafer-Landau presents an interesting dilemma for the moral education theorist regarding the conception of autonomy. He says that either autonomy may sometimes be permissibly infringed, or it may not. The first horn becomes a slippery slope if one assumes that punishment is autonomy infringement, yet is sometimes justified. In that case, it would be difficult to distinguish cases of punishment when autonomy infringement is justified and when it is not (Shafer-Landau, 195-196).

The second horn, that autonomy infringement is never permissible, is the one that most modern moral education theorists, such as Morris and myself, adopt. Shafer-Landau says that taking this horn requires, firstly, explaining why punishment is not a limitation on autonomy. Secondly, this horn requires an argument for the existence of an inalienable right to moral autonomy or for an "exceptionless prohibition on autonomy infringement" (196). Thirdly, this horn requires an argument "to dissolve the apparent tension between an attachment to autonomy and the belief in inalienable rights, since inalienable rights specify restrictions on the autonomy of rights holders" (196).

Punishment is not an infringement of moral autonomy. Moral autonomy only involves the freedom to choose (or reject) the good. In being punished for an offense by means of probation, fines, or incarceration, an offender is not being forced to choose the good. His will is not being manipulated simply because his body is not free and his range of possible actions is limited. In contrast, if punishment entailed psychosurgery or some form of brainwashing to mold the will to accept certain values, then the offender's moral autonomy would be infringed. Offenders in these cases would not be capable of carefully considering the reasons why moral ends are good to have, and their treatment could not be regarded as justified.

Shafer-Landau's second concern is more problematic. Morris has claimed that we cannot waive our right to be treated as a moral person because such a waiver would not morally permit another to treat us as less than human. While this response has been regarded as question begging by Shafer-Landau, I think that Morris is implying (though not completely clarifying) that moral autonomy or the freedom to choose the good is a human feature which gives us essential value. For instance, if I were to give up this freedom by consenting to a form of psychosurgery in which I lost all capacity to make moral determinations, then I would have lost that feature about myself which gives me my greatest value both for myself and for others. Without that feature, I would have no more value than an animal and would have no right to be treated differently than an animal. No one has the right to treat me as less than human (or morally autonomous) while I remain morally autonomous, even when I foolishly consider waiving my right to moral autonomy by having drastic psychosurgery.

The assertion that moral autonomy is my most valuable feature is grounded in the arguments of Edmund Pincoffs and, especially, John Rawls. Pincoffs defends the value of the "mandatory moral virtues," which have to do with not taking advantage of others and the "non-mandatory moral virtues," which refer to a concern for the interests of others. Pincoffs claims that having these virtues means that one's company will be preferred, and that not having them will mean one is likely to be avoided. If a person lacks even the mandatory moral virtues, she will not be regarded as a member of the moral community, and there will be few circumstances in which he or she will be chosen or preferred. Having both the non-mandatory and mandatory moral virtues, on the other hand, will cause one to be favored and sought after by other members of the moral community (Pincoffs, 180-182).

Rawls finds a strong basis for the value of having moral ends in his argument that the virtues are excellences. First, Rawls argues that a person is judged to be good by others either because he has some property held to be of instrumental value or because he has the basic moral virtues, which includes a sense of justice. It is rational for members of a well-ordered society to want other members of their society to have the moral virtues, which for Rawls are sentiments and habitual attitudes leading persons to act on principles of right. It is rational to want the moral virtues in others because the morally virtuous will act to advance the good (the rational plans) of others (Rawls, 434-438).

Secondly, Rawls claims the most important primary good is self-respect, which is essential for persons to satisfy their basic desire to utilize and maximize their talents (the Aristotelian Principle). Self-respect includes a person's sense of his own value, the sense that his plan of life is worth carrying out, and confidence in his abilities to fulfill his intentions. To have self-respect a person must have a rational plan of life, and he must find his person and activities appreciated and confirmed by others whom he esteems and whose association he enjoys. A person acquires a sense of worth through the esteem of others for his activities. His associative ties reduce the likelihood of failure and provide support against self-doubt when mishaps occur. Thus, we see that self-respect, which is necessary to pursue any rational plan, requires social support (Rawls, 440-441).

From the preceding, it may be argued that one need not have moral worth to receive the social support which is essential to one's self-respect. Persons may simply have properties that others find pleasant, such as being witty or handsome. However, the preceding is only part of Rawls' argument that the virtues are excellences. The rest of the argument pertains to the establishment of moral principles and the basis of the human desire to act on these principles.

Rawls claims that "the Kantian interpretation of the original position means that the desire to do what is right and just is the main way for persons to express their nature as free and equal rational beings" (445). The original position refers to the position from which rational and mutually disinterested persons can be expected to choose correct principles of justice. All persons in the original position are under a veil of ignorance as to their subjective desires and actual situation in life. They are free of the bias their particular circumstances and desires would create in the choice of principles, and they are equally in ignorance of their particular circumstances. They are simply guided by a concern for how they would like to be treated if they found themselves in any given social and natural situation. When persons act on the basis of such principles, Rawls argues, they are expressing their nature as free and equal rational beings subject to the general conditions of human life. "For to express one's nature as a being of a particular kind is to act on the principles that would be chosen if this nature were the decisive determining element" (Rawls, 253). To act on such principles, Rawls further argues, is to act on Kantian categorical imperatives. Kant says that we must act only on maxims that are universalizable or acceptable to anyone regardless of her subjective interests and situation. For Kant, it is a special feature of human nature that humans have the capacity to act on such maxims, and only in such acting do humans truly express their freedom, which can be construed as both freedom from purely contingent desires and freedom to act in accordance with self-chosen principles (Rawls, 251-257).

To complete his argument, Rawls refers again to the Aristotelian Principle. It can be said that the capacity to act purely on objective interests, or the interests one has from the standpoint of the original position, is innate in human beings. It is an innate capacity which when exercised most fully expresses human freedom and rationality. If humans do enjoy exercising their innate abilities, and if they gain greater enjoyment as their skills increase and the complexity of the exercises increase, then it must be the case that they will desire to exercise this innate ability to act solely on moral principle. Rawls acknowledges that persons desire to exercise certain talents more than others, but the talents they choose to exercise are typically those that other persons most value in us. Thus, Rawls argues that the moral virtues and their exercise are excellences valued by ourselves as well as others. They are means for achieving social support and self-respect.

Clearly, Rawls' argument rests on the truth of the Aristotelian principle, which Rawls holds to be a deep psychological fact about human nature. Given that humans desire to flourish and improve their talents, there appears to be a legitimate basis for accepting the value to all humans of moral autonomy. Of course, Shafer-Landau wonders if the most "hard-bitten criminal" is capable of choosing the good. In view of my description of the psychopathic offender, his concern is not a problem. The psychopathic offender is still capable of choosing moral means even if he is never likely to choose moral ends. He can still acquire the mandatory moral virtues, in Pincoffs' terms.

The third problem in taking the second horn of Shafer-Landau's dilemma is that if we claim that moral autonomy is an inalienable right, then we are not free to give up our moral freedom. If we are not free to waive it, one must explain in what sense we are free. Resolving this problem requires distinctions in forms of autonomy, which I will address in the chapter on self-determination. At this stage I will only say that this problem can be answered by consideration of the process of moral development or how freedom is acquired through human maturation.

In this section I have distinguished my moral education account from Kantian retributivism, while indicating their common grounding in the inviolability and worth of moral autonomy. Kantian retributivism is insufficient as a justification for punishment because it does not account for human flourishing and the basic desire in each of us to grow and live well and to see our fellows also live well. Desert alone is an insufficient justification for punishment because it is only backward-looking. Desert does not consider what people are capable of becoming and capable of desiring. Desert ignores the future potentialities of persons and the value they can be to us. Of course, Kantian retributivists, such as Rawls, try to be forward-looking when they say that deterrence is an important consideration for legislators when determining general punishments for certain classes of crimes. They simply think that individual punishments as determined by the judiciary are justified by desert alone. In doing so, however, they ignore the value of the rational potential of all persons who are punished.

SELF-PROTECTION

I have suggested that adding Warren Quinn's justification of punishment as self-protection to the moral education account would create a satisfactory comprehensive theory. The advantage of the self-protection account is that it values the good (the safety and security) of society and victims of offenses. It is chiefly concerned with the good of potential victims and society at large, while the moral education account concentrates on the benefits to the wrongdoer. It can be said, however, that the self-protection account has some regard for the wrongdoer in that it respects his rationality by giving him reasons not to offend. It can also be said that moral education theory has regard for victims and society because a morally reformed person is less likely to commit offenses against others in the future. However, in both theories the benefits to those persons with whom the theory is not primarily concerned are achieved only indirectly. I believe that a satisfactory theory of the justification of punishment should give direct consideration to all persons affected by the act of punishing.

One objection to this view comes from Libertarian political philosophers, who claim that self-protection is the only justification for punishment. Jeffrie Murphy has argued that Libertarianism is opposed to the moral education justification of punishment because Libertarianism believes that it is not the business of government to impose on individuals its own vision of the good life. Since moral education theory thinks the state is communicating correct values in justly punishing, Murphy believes these two positions must be at odds. This constitutes an important objection to moral education theory because Libertarianism is a widely accepted political theory. In this section I will address this objection to moral education or the view that a belief in Libertarian political philosophy requires one to believe that self-protection is not only necessary and sufficient for punishing but also that self-protection is the only proper reason for punishing. I will also address objections from Shafer-Landau pertaining to the feasibility of the hybrid theory I am proposing.

There are reasons to believe that Murphy is wrong, and Libertarianism need not conflict with a concern for the moral education of those we punish. To show the compatibility of these positions, I present the ideas of a radical Libertarian philosopher and psychiatrist. I show that his conception of the sole good, liberty, is compatible with the value of morally educating by means of punishment. I also argue that insofar as Libertarianism dictates that laws are justified by the principle of harm, Libertarianism cannot avoid endorsing laws that communicate some conception of the good.

Peter Breggin expresses a classic Libertarian position in his book, *The Psychology of Freedom*, which is at least superficially in direct contradiction to moral education theory, while he does not explicitly reject the concept. He claims that Libertarians believe in freedom of action and thought and in free will. They believe that persons reach their full potential through the development and use of reason. Given the capacity to choose and to reason, all humans have the right to express their choices and reasoning processes through action. Ethical conduct, for the Libertarian, is conduct "consistent with rationally self-determined ideals or values" (Breggin, 57). Thus, we may never use force against people who act badly except in defense of our own liberty or the liberty of others (Breggin, 56-57).

From the foregoing, Breggin seems to be advocating an ethical view much like that of Ayn Rand and other ethical egoists, who find no intrinsic value in altruistic behavior. However, his full view is more consistent with the virtue theories of those philosophers who explicitly endorse moral education.

Breggin clarifies his concept of unethical acts when he speaks of "The Paradox of Liberty and Love." Breggin says that love makes existence worthwhile, and the "ultimate of personal sovereignty is the awareness of one's capacity to love and the ultimate in personal freedom is the opportunity to express and share this love" (Breggin, 219). To be a free person in Breggin's view is not to be lonely or isolated, but to be deeply involved in life and with others. Thus, Breggin seems to be endorsing a variant of virtue theory in the sense that freedom, for him the sole moral value, should be exercised to establish a loving kinship with others, which we should all seek in order to live well.

Granted, Breggin advocates a loving environment rather than force as a means of morally educating children, but only because love is more respectful of the child's rationality and autonomy. By force, Breggin is specifically speaking of controlling behavior via Skinnerian means in disregard of the person's rational capacities. In fact, in denouncing "moral authority," he refers to such authority as "always oppressive" and as "any individual, group, or institution that seeks to control others by means of emotional, psychological, or spiritual pressure and manipulation" (Breggin, 233). He deplores such attempts at control, whether they are by means of rewards or punishments. He does not, however, categorically deplore punishment or the setting of limits on anyone as a means of self-protection.

In deploring oppressive means of control, Breggin agrees with my moral education account, which does not tolerate abuse of a person's rational autonomy. This moral education view sees punishment as communicating that there are moral limits to behavior. It helps the offender to understand that certain behavior is clearly detrimental to her well-being. It is a sort of "tough love" which both protects the victim and potential victims and improves the offender's life through helping her reconnect with other persons. In helping her reconnect, it can help her achieve the sort of freedom that Breggin endorses as the only good.

In regards to the issue of the compatibility of Libertarianism and moral education, Richard Tur has argued that the Libertarian goal of the "moral disestablishment" of systems of laws is impossible. By "moral disestablishment," Tur means that Libertarians like Mill believe that a correct system of laws will not dictate morality to individuals governed by those laws. Rather, Libertarians believe that the harm principle is the only legitimate basis for laws that will interfere with individual freedom. The harm principle sanctions only those laws that prohibit harm to others and to essential social institutions. If Tur is correct, then Libertarianism and moral education may not be incompatible since both are concerned with maximizing the rational autonomy of individuals.

Richard Tur (with the help of Neil MacCormick) argues that the harm principle posits two conflicting values and that disestablishmentarians cannot reconcile these values without a clearer conception of the good. Tur says that "the harm principle presupposes a prior determination of legitimate private interest and a conception of the public good" (Tur, 178). He presents several interesting cases of prosecuted assaults in which the victims apparently consented to being assaulted. One was a beggar who asked a friend to cut off his hand to make him look more pathetic to patrons. Another was a prostitute who offered sadomasochistic sexual activities to customers. In both cases, the victims of assault acquiesced and in fact solicited the assaults. In both cases the assaults were prosecuted. The harm principle, it would appear, supports these prosecutions because the victims were harmed even though they chose to be harmed and because the public good is harmed by the existence of beggars and brothels.

Of course, Libertarians may argue that the freedom to choose is paramount, even the freedom to choose to be harmed. Thus, they may disagree with the prosecutions of these cases. The consequence, however, is that they would endorse the freedom to choose to give up one's freedom to choose, perhaps including by means of drastic psychosurgery. This choice is one that Mill famously will not allow, but Mill has been criticized for making an ad hoc move in restricting freedom in this way. The point essentially is that anyone who endorses the harm principle as the justification for law must have some conception of when suffering harm is legitimately chosen and when it is not, and this necessarily involves some notion of the good. For Mill, the good at least pertains to which harms it is *rational* to choose.

My moral education account, which views punishment as a means for appealing to the prudential rationality of offenders, is not incompatible with the Libertarian position, which is exemplified by Mill. Mill clearly values *rational* autonomy. My account values rational autonomy and sees punishment as a means of promoting it, while also accepting the necessity of self-protection as another justification for punishing.

My account of a comprehensive theory is, of course, a hybrid account, and Shafer-Landau describes several objections to moral education as a part of such an account. He says that in constructing any hybrid theory a problem can arise with the proper assignment of weights to each strand of the theory. I am inclined to believe that moral education and self-protection should be given equal weight. Both the wrongdoer and others who are affected by his offense should have their good directly taken into account for punishment to be justified. Giving the two strands equal weight, however, is problematic if they can come into conflict.

Some accounts of the justification of punishment clearly conflict with other accounts. For instance, as Shafer-Landau suggests, we may wonder about a case where "we allow a criminal's moral education to be sacrificed in a well-publicized case with lots of deterrent capacity" (218). Shafer-Landau is correct that deterrence theory with its potential for abuses of justice comes into conflict with many other theories. There is no need, however, to worry about competition between the goals of self-protection and moral education. Both theories appeal to the rationality of the wrongdoers in justifying punishment. Only if punishment can be a reason for a person not to commit a crime are we justified in punishing that person, according to Quinn's theory. Only if a person is sufficiently rational to comprehend the value of taking only moral means are we justified in punishing according to my moral education account. Both theories are respectful of the offender's rationality.

It can be objected that the self-protection account may lead to excessively long sentences for certain offenses that the moral education account would not countenance. For instance, there seems to be nothing in this account that would prevent twenty-year sentences for shoplifting because a sentence of this length would constitute a very strong reason not to shoplift, which could consequently result in greater protection for shop owners. Quinn, however, shows that his self-protection account can be sensitive to the concern of the moral education theorist. While punishment is meant by self-protection to be a reason not to commit a crime, Quinn says that not every degree of punishment may be imposed for any crime because morality regards the criminal as not fully competent (only rational in a limited sense) in his capacity to dispose of the whole of himself and his life (Quinn, 67). In other words, to be subject to punishment the wrongdoer must be able to understand that the punishment is a reason for him to not commit the offense. If the reason is not understood by him sufficiently to deter him, then he is insufficiently rational to understand his true good and consequently in need of paternalistic regard by those who punish him.

There are reasons to believe that both moral education and self-protection are necessary parts of the justification of punishment. Libertarians, who typically endorse only self-protection, need not object to my moral education account, which is fully respectful of the offender's rational autonomy. Further, Libertarians may implicitly endorse moral education when they consider what freedom fully entails. Self-protection and moral education are compatible reasons for punishing that need not come into conflict because they both rely on the rationality of the offender in justifying punishment. However, self-protection alone is not sufficient to justify any form of punishing because it can support excessive punishments and because it is not directly concerned with benefiting the person punishment effects the most, the offender.

THE PRACTICALITY OF MORAL EDUCATION

While I addressed some objections related to the practicality of moral education in the section on deterrence, there remain other objections to moral education related to the practicality issue. The theory must be practical because if punishment cannot reasonably be expected to educate morally, then either moral education is not necessary to justify punishment or punishment cannot be justified. In other words, even if punishment cannot be adequately justified by deterrence, Kantian retributivism, or self-protection alone, it is possible that moral education is not necessary to justify punishment. It does not contribute to the justification if it does not occur.

While endorsing his own program of moral education, Duff expresses some concerns about its feasibility which lead him to worry that we must fall back on deterrence to justify our current practices of punishment. Nigel Walker doubts that moral education occurs often enough to be a practical goal. In terms of sentencing policies, it has been objected that the goal of moral education may be self-defeating. In this section I will address each of these practical concerns about moral education.

In *Trials and Punishments* Duff defends a conception of the common good which just laws are designed to uphold. It involves certain core values which all of the members of a society share. Punishment in Duff's view is meant to promote acceptance of these core values by offenders. He acknowledges that this is an ideal conception of punishment and may not be feasible for our existing penal system. Duff states that

> insofar as the society in which the offender lives does not constitute a genuine community, united by shared values and mutual concern and respect; insofar as the laws which claim to bind her cannot be adequately justified to her; neither her crime nor her punishment can have the meaning which this account ascribes to them (292).

While Duff does not elaborate on specific problems with our existing penal system, I imagine that he is referring to inequities in how punishment is meted out and to the sorry state of many of our prisons. Considerable discrepancies in punishments for like offenses, discriminatory practices in the prosecutions of certain crimes and certain offenders, and prison environments that seem purely coercive can negate the possibility of moral education.

I think that with the more limited view of moral education that I propose moral reform is a viable goal even within our troubled penal system. For instance, while an offender may be reasonably resentful if she is incarcerated for a lengthier period than another person who committed a worse offense but who could afford a better lawyer, her resentment need not stand in the way of her acknowledging that she did commit a crime for which she deserves some punishment. Simply because some aspects of her punishment are unjust, it does not follow that her punishment is completely unjust. Further, if our prisons are more oriented toward coercion than rehabilitation, they may at least elicit the regret that is needed to prompt an offender to consider a change in her behavior. Some individuals may only require the experience of suffering in return for their offense to realize that they need to make character changes. While moral education would surely be promoted if all prisons emphasized rehabilitation, the prison experience as it is now does in many cases influence the prudentially rational offender to reconsider her present value system.

Walker raises two questions for the moral education theorist. He asks first whether moral reform takes place often enough to make it reasonable to hope for repentance. Secondly, he asks whether we can punish those we know to be incapable of moral improvement.

I intend to more fully address Walker's first question in a later chapter where I explore some of the correctional counseling literature related to those goals that correctional counselors have deemed capable of being achieved. Walker's second question relates specifically to my earlier discussion about the psychopathic offender. Insofar as even the psychopath is capable of being rational in a limited sense (i.e., prudentially), he does seem to be susceptible to some moral reform. As long as he can learn it is in his best interest to obey society's moral dictates he can be reformed and benefited, and it is consequently legitimate to punish him.

Yet another practical objection to moral education relates to whether moral education requires determinate sentences for all crimes of a like nature or indeterminate sentences. Under a determinate sentencing policy, all persons convicted of a particular offense receive the same fixed sentence. For example, with this policy, if five years is designated as the proper punishment for burglary, then any person convicted of burglary would be given a five-year sentence and would not be released until exactly five years had expired. Under an indeterminate sentencing policy, convicted offenders are given a sentence range specifying a minimum and a maximum amount of time to be served in prison. For example, if a range of three to ten years is designated as a proper range for burglary, then any person convicted of burglary is given a three- to ten-year sentence. A person convicted of burglary under this type of indeterminate sentence who behaved well in prison and cooperated with recommended rehabilitative programs would probably be released with the permission of the parole board after three years. A convicted burglar who did not behave well and who refused to participate in rehabilitative programs would probably serve the full ten years if the parole board believed there was no justification for his poor behavior and refusal.

Hampton and Duff both maintain that the moral education account requires determinate sentencing. Shafer-Landau claims that the moral education account requires indeterminate sentencing. All three philosophers appear to believe that determinate sentencing is to be preferred to indeterminate sentencing. They appear to believe that indeterminate sentencing is unjust and unduly coercive and that the personal autonomy of the offender is violated when he is denied the right to refuse to be morally rehabilitated. Thus, Shafer-Landau objects that moral education theory requires a form of sentencing which is unjust and violates personal autonomy, while Hampton and Duff believe the theory does not require a form of sentencing which they also deplore.

In their condemnation of indeterminate sentencing, Hampton, Duff, and Shafer-Landau are dismissive of the views of Karl Menninger, a strong early advocate of indeterminate sentencing. Menninger believes that it is not to the benefit of an offender to release him from prison before he has the opportunity to acquire the skills requisite for surviving in the community. Without these skills, we are condemning the offender to almost certain recidivism. Thus, Menninger thinks we owe it to the offender to lengthen his stay to insure the probability of his success upon release. Of course, Menninger does not take into account that this would condemn especially recalcitrant offenders to sentences quite extraordinary for their crimes. Nevertheless, I think that Menninger voices some concerns about determinate sentencing that moral education theorists should not neglect.

I have had occasion in working with the Kansas Department of Corrections from 1987 when an indeterminate sentencing policy was in effect through the early 1990s when a determinate sentencing policy became state law to consider the advantages and disadvantages of both forms. A number of states reversed their sentencing policies in the 1980s and 1990s apparently in response to concerns arising from studies suggesting that prison rehabilitative programs were not working, concerns related to racially discriminatory judicial sentencing for like offenses, and concerns that enforced participation in rehabilitative programs had been counterproductive. It may be significant that Hampton, Duff, and Shafer-Landau expressed their views against indeterminate sentencing during this period of a shift in correctional philosophy.

It is my position that moral education theory need not endorse either determinate or indeterminate sentencing as it has been practiced in the past. Rather, I propose that the most defensible form of sentencing, and one which moral education can support, would be a modified determinate or a mixed determinate–indeterminate sentencing policy. Such a policy could avoid the drawbacks of strictly determinate and indeterminate sentencing policies while taking into account concerns for justice and respect for the needs of the individual offender. It does not have to be the case that in sentencing either justice is respected or the individual rehabilitative needs of the offender are addressed, but not both.

To elucidate my position, I will cite specific cases (real and hypothetical) in which either strictly determinate or strictly indeterminate sentencing are clearly detrimental. An associate of mine was involved in psychologically evaluating a felon who was sentenced under indeterminate sentencing to five years to life for a violent offense, which I recall as an aggravated burglary. He was a recidivist, and I imagine that the judge in sentencing this man was particularly concerned to require his rehabilitation prior to parole. When my associate interviewed this man for a parole evaluation, he had already served twenty years in prison. He had already exceeded by at least ten years the normal length of incarceration for persons who had committed like offenses. Unfortunately, this person showed no signs of remorse during his parole evaluation and expressed the intention of reoffending upon release. His psychological profile also showed a high probability for reoffending. He had been placed in rehabilitative programs but had performed poorly. Subsequently, I learned that this man was released into the community shortly after determinate sentencing went into effect in Kansas. I did not have the opportunity to learn whether he committed further crimes. While it seems highly probable that he did, his punishment was clearly excessive for his offense. In being excessive, it did not communicate the correct moral message to him. As Duff states, if our aim in punishing is to communicate the nature and implications of an offense and to persuade an offender that the punishment is appropriate to the offense, then we must not punish indefinitely (Duff, 278).

Determinate sentencing, which is the sentencing of persons who have committed like offenses to identical terms in prison, also has its problems. Because it ignores the differences in rehabilitation potential of offenders, Shafer-Landau thinks moral education theory cannot endorse it. Take the case of a drunk driver who has been convicted ten times for driving under the influence (DUI) and who has been sentenced to two years in prison. Under determinate sentencing this individual has no external incentive to attend a substance abuse treatment program, AA meetings, or alcohol education classes because he will not be disadvantaged for not addressing his alcoholism. A convicted pedophile will similarly have no external incentive to attend sex offender treatment under determinate sentencing. In these cases it seems highly detrimental to both the public and the inmates not to require participation (or at least the physical presence of the inmates) in important rehabilitative programs.

It has been argued that prison rehabilitative programs have minimal success and that inmates who are coerced into attending these programs do not benefit. The latter claim has been contradicted by reports of rehabilitative treatment staff. Some sex offender counselors have informed me personally that they have worked with sex offenders who, while initially resistant to the program, over time came to acknowledge their sexual offenses and to actively participate in the treatment process. In the case of the repeated DUI offender who is highly resistant to attending substance abuse treatment, enforced participation in at least an alcohol education class cannot be construed as either unduly coercive or not to his benefit. In an alcohol education class the DUI offender is educated in the signs of alcoholism and in alternative methods for achieving sobriety. Simply requiring his physical presence in a classroom where he cannot avoid hearing information about the signs and treatment of alcoholism does not violate, or illegitimately limit, his personal autonomy. It is not a case of a violation of personal autonomy because the offender retains the ability to refuse to learn anything from this experience. It is not a violation of his autonomy any more than reprimanding a person for bad behavior violates her autonomy. It is not a violation of his autonomy because the offender retains the capacity to choose what is good or bad for him. His autonomy in this case would only be violated if he had been unjustly convicted of his multiple DUIs or if the class employed some sort of brainwashing exercise or psychosurgery that effectively molded his will.

The sentencing policy that I propose takes into account both concerns for justice and individual differences in inmates. When determinate sentencing began in Kansas, a number of correctional officers protested that under the new system inmates would have no real incentive for behaving themselves while in prison. Consequently, the legislature made a minor modification in the new sentencing policy to allow up to sixty days' early release for good behavior. I am proposing a further modification to encourage inmates to participate in vital rehabilitative programs. By vital rehabilitative programs, I am referring to programs addressing problems that are identified as directly causative of an offense. Sentences could be reduced by six months to a year under the provision that an offender who, for instance, has been diagnosed as having a substance abuse problem and whose offense is substance abuse related attend a substance abuse treatment program. Sex offenders would be given the incentive of early release for attending sex offender treatment. Possibly offenders who fail to pay child support because of a lack of work skills would be given the incentive of early release for completing GED classes or a short vocational training course.

As Duff has argued, there are conventional standards of sentencing that the public at large acknowledges as just for certain types of offenses. Conventional standards vary between states to a minor extent, but variations of a year or two in sentencing like offenses are not typically objected to as unjust. Convention supports the decisions of judges to modify sentences slightly due to mitigating and aggravating factors involved in offenses. Consequently, evidence of the intention to make permanent improvements in oneself by participating in prison rehabilitation programs is surely a reasonable basis for making at least minor reductions in sentencing.

I believe that this proposal promotes the aims of the moral education justification of punishment. The moral education justification requires that punishment be a response to an offense and consequently should be proportional to that offense. It is also concerned with punishment as a means of benefiting the offender by promoting moral reform. Rehabilitative programs promote permanent reform, and thus moral education theory must promote such programs. Further, moral education does not necessitate either determinate sentencing or indeterminate sentencing as they have been practiced in the past. Rather, moral education requires both that justice be done in sentencing and that the rehabilitative needs of offenders be met. Correct sentencing policies can meet both of these concerns. Hence, moral education is not proven to be impractical in terms of the type of sentencing policy it requires.

The foregoing indicates that moral education is a practical goal of punishment. Given the more limited goals of my moral education account, the practicality objections are readily answered. On my account, as long as punishment suffices to convince persons of the need to take only moral means toward their ends, moral education is accomplished. Insofar as punishment in the form of incarceration induces suffering and is a consequence of violations of just laws, prisoners who are prudentially rational should be capable of being convinced. If they cannot be convinced, they should not be punished.

In arguing for the necessity of moral education in this chapter, I have not tried to prove the sufficiency of self-protection and moral education together as the two constituents of a comprehensive theory. Some may argue that deterrence or Kantian retributivism can work as well in combination with moral education to justify punishment. Quinn has provided a fairly convincing argument that self-protection can adequately replace the two standard accounts, and I have nothing to add to his claims. For the purpose of elucidating a specific goal of correction counseling, it is enough to prove that moral education is an important and necessary function of punishment.

Chapter Three

Justifying the
Paternalism of Punishing

Morris describes the moral education account of the justification of punishment as paternalistic. The reader may note that I concur with Morris when I refer in chapter 2 to the enforcement of just laws as a justifiable paternalism because it promotes rational behavior. Further explanation, however, is needed to clarify what I mean by paternalism and, more specifically, paternalism by the state and how it is when it is justified. In other words, if the moral education account requires state paternalism, then an explanation and justification of why the state may act paternalistically toward those it punishes is needed. This is required not only in defense of the moral education account but also in defense of self-determination as a goal of correctional counseling. Punishment must be seen as a good for persons who are punished if it is capable of facilitating the therapeutic goal of enhancing autonomy.

In this chapter I will address the issue of paternalism by considering the merits of one particular definition of paternalism and examining several current justifications of this type of behavior. I do not intend to review all of the definitions that have been proposed because my aim is chiefly to ascertain why different contemporary philosophers perceive paternalistic behavior to be in need of justification. I intend to consider what gives paternalism its negative value by exploring possible objections and counterexamples to this definition. In terms of the justifications of paternalistic acts, the main differences seem to rest on beliefs in the correctness of either a deontological or a consequentialist normative standard for evaluating behavior. I think that there are advantages in the use of both standards for the justification of paternalism. I think that a fully adequate justification should respect the implicit values associated with each.

In what follows I present and defend a simple working definition of paternalism suggested by Gerald Dworkin. I also explain its utility for justifying state paternalism. Secondly, I consider several competing justifications for paternalistic acts from deontological and consequentialist ethical positions in order to determine the true substantive values which a correct justification of paternalism must rely on. I conclude by exploring the distinction between individual and state paternalism and describe how the state paternalism of punishment is specifically justified.

DEFINING PATERNALISM

For the purpose of examining the permissibility of state punishment for the purpose of moral education, I am adopting Dworkin's most recent definition of paternalism. It has the virtue of being fairly simple, and it is inclusive enough to cover punishing for the purpose of moral education. Dworkin says that P acts paternalistically toward Q if and only if (a) P acts with the intent of averting some harm or promoting some benefit for Q; (b) P acts contrary to (or is indifferent to) the current preferences, desires, or values of Q; and (c) P's act is a limitation on Q's autonomy or liberty (Dworkin 1995, 564). By the moral education account, punishment is intended to be a benefit to the person punished, it is inflicted regardless of his preferences, desires, or values, and it limits his freedom of action.

Dworkin's first condition is commonly found in philosophical conceptions of paternalism. The idea that the paternalist intends to benefit in some way the person she acts on is also found in the definitions of paternalism stated by Paul Hershey, John Kultgen, Charles Culver and Bernard Gert, and David Archard. However, a broader conception of paternalism, which eschews this condition, can be found in *Webster's Collegiate Dictionary*, 10th edition. In *Webster's,* a paternalistic action is one in which an authority (presumably any person who has the ability to take such action) acts to supply the needs or regulate the conduct of other persons under her control in terms of matters that impact those persons and others whom they are in some relationship with. This definition is broader because it can include disciplinary actions not motivated by an interest in benefiting the person acted on.

The *Webster's* definition seems consistent with the broader sense of the word "paternal" as acting "like a father" because fathers can be good or bad toward those in their charge. The good fathers are those who correct, discipline, or otherwise intervene in their children's lives for the children's future welfare. When disciplining, good fathers mean to teach the child how to relate well with others so that the child can live a happier life. Bad fathers discipline for no other reason than to keep the child under control for the father's own benefit or for the benefit of others whom the child interacts with. They are bad fathers because they are indifferent or hostile toward the child who is dependent on them. This indifference or hostility can cause substantial damage to a child's self-esteem and future prospects.

I expect that philosophers who are interested in formulating a correct definition typically do not include actions in order to regulate conduct without regard for the recipient's benefit because they believe that being a father toward someone in any sense besides a pure biological relation requires having some concern for him. Of course, it is possible that even a good father may on occasion discipline a child only from the desire to control him. Yet in those situations, he may not be regarded as acting in a fatherly manner. Rather, he may be regarded as being, at least temporarily, a tyrant. Insofar as being a father means that one generally acts toward one's offspring out of concern for their welfare, it is correct to limit paternalistic behavior in this manner.

Dworkin's second condition, that *P*'s action is contrary *or* indifferent to the current preferences, desires, or values of *Q*, is consistent with disparate views of philosophers regarding the importance of consent. Put in terms of Dworkin's symbols, Kultgen says that a necessary condition of parentalistic (his gender-neutral equivalent to paternalism) acts is that *P* decides to perform the action independently of whether *Q* authorizes the action at the time of the performance (Kultgen, 62). Again using Dworkin's symbols, Hershey says that a necessary condition is that *Q*'s consent or dissent is not a relevant consideration for *P* (179). Dworkin's word indifference captures the disregard for *Q*'s present consent connoted by these two definitions. While indifference sometimes also has an affectual connotation that

Kultgen and Hershey do not intend, its simplest meaning reflects not making a difference, which does not have any affectual connotation. When persons make choices, they consider certain factors. They do not consider other factors, not because they disvalue them, but only because those factors are judged not relevant to their decision. Those other factors make no difference in their decision. Kultgen and Hershey agree that Q's consent makes no difference or is not relevant to the paternalist (parentalist) when she acts in terms of changing her decision. Thus, Dworkin captures in this second condition some of the flavor of Kultgen's and Hershey's definitions.

Dworkin's second condition also captures some of the essence of Archard's definition of paternalism as the usurpation (or overturning) of a person's present choices or will by another with a view to promoting that person's interest or good (Archard, 341). If paternalism usurps a subject's present choices, then it may well be contrary to his own choices. Insofar as a person's choices express his values, his values (beliefs about his own good) will also be usurped, and the paternalist will act on beliefs about what is good for the subject that are contrary to the subject's beliefs. In including the possibility that the choices, values, and preferences of the paternalist and her subject regarding the subject's good can be contrary, I think that Dworkin is trying to accommodate the intuitions of persons like Archard.

In an earlier essay, Dworkin provided a necessary condition for paternalism that is somewhat similar to Archard's. Dworkin said at that time that paternalism necessarily involves an attempt to substitute one person's judgment for another, to promote the latter's benefit (Dworkin 1983b, 107). An attempt to substitute judgment also suggests that the person acted on may have different (and even contrary) choices, values, and preferences than the paternalist in regard to the person's welfare. While a substitution of judgment does not necessarily indicate contrary values in the paternalist and her subject (and perhaps not as strongly as usurpation), I think it likely that Dworkin is interested in accommodating the different intuitions of philosophers such as Archard, Kultgen, and Hershey regarding the paternalist's attitude toward her subject. In capturing these different intuitions, I think Dworkin's definition has a broad appeal.

Dworkin's latest definition does not make specific reference to a substitution of judgment, but his third condition seems to capture that idea in requiring that the act in some way limit the subject's autonomy. His third condition is probably the most controversial, yet I think it also has some advantages for my examination of state paternalism. For one, it limits the kind of beings that we can be paternalistic toward.

This limitation is not found in the definitions of Hershey and Kultgen. In their definitions, the person acted on must be capable of being benefited (or at least the paternalist must believe her to have that capacity), and this is the only property that she must have. In consequence, Hershey and Kultgen's definitions allow us to be paternalistic toward the comatose and other beings that are temporarily or permanently nonrational, such as animals. Since the consent of the individual acted on is not always a relevant consideration for the paternalist according to both Hershey and Kultgen, it is sometimes irrelevant whether that individual is in any respect capable of giving consent. In this respect, they are at odds with Archard, Dworkin, and Culver and Gert.

While the ability to give consent is implied in Archard's and Dworkin's definitions, Culver and Gert specifically claim that the person acted on must be capable of giving simple or valid consent. Simple consent, which is less stringent than valid consent, requires noncoercion but only a limited or insubstantial capacity to comprehend or appreciate information regarding the consequences of being acted on. The permanently comatose, infants, and animals are not capable of giving simple consent, but Culver and Gert do not believe that anyone acts paternalistically toward those individuals. Rather, they maintain that a paternalistic action always has negative connotations. No one disapproves of trying to benefit nonrational beings without their consent. They also believe in a rule-based morality. So a paternalistic action in their view must always involve a moral rule violation.

In claiming that the person who is paternalistically acted on has her choices usurped or another's judgment substituted for hers, Dworkin and Archard indicate that the person acted on is a being who can make choices or has a capacity to judge. They agree in seeing a paternalistic act as in some respect infringing on or limiting a person's autonomy. Insofar as autonomy is considered a universal human good, they also build into their definitions a negative value for paternalism.

Culver and Gert, however, do not agree that paternalism must infringe on autonomy. They think that the moral rule, "Don't deprive of freedom," is simply one rule among a number of others that can be violated when a person acts paternalistically. They refer to several apparent cases of paternalism, which do not involve a restriction on freedom, but which are paternalistic (according to their definition) because they violate other moral rules. I think, however, that these cases all involve some sort of limitation on autonomy. As I will show, all of these purported counterexamples to Dworkin's definition are unconvincing.

Firstly, Culver and Gert present a case of giving a blood transfusion to an unconscious person, who had previously expressed a religious belief in the prohibition of blood transfusions to keep persons alive (127). They indicate that this clearly paternalistic act does not interfere with the person's freedom because he cannot act and he is incapable of choosing or judging when he is acted on. I think, however, that this action can be construed as limiting the person's autonomy because in giving him the blood transfusion the paternalistic doctor is substituting his own judgment for the judgment of the patient at the time when he was conscious. In Archard's terms, the patient's choices are overturned even though they were not made at the moment of the paternalistic action. The comatose patient has no opportunity to refuse, but it seems very likely that he would refuse had he been conscious at the time. The doctor has no reason to believe that the patient would change his mind on this issue. His past choice in this case seems as representative of his true wishes as would be his present choice given the unlikely possibility that he would momentarily wake up from his coma to refuse the transfusion. In giving him the transfusion, the doctor is clearly not respecting the patient's choice.

Secondly, Culver and Gert bring up the case of a doctor who lies to a mother on her deathbed about the fate of her son, who has just been killed during an attempted escape from prison (128). To ease her death, she tells the mother that the son is doing well. Culver and Gert claim that the doctor is breaking the moral rule not to deceive, but she is not coercing the mother, not controlling her behavior, and not interfering with her liberty of action. While it may seem a stretch to call this case a limitation on autonomy, I think that it can be described as such. While the mother is incapable of acting, she remains capable of thinking and of choosing how to regard her life. The doctor is denying her the freedom to view her past negatively. She is denying the mother knowledge of the truth because she values the mother's happiness higher than her self-knowledge, at least in this instance. This action seems intuitively justified because most of us would not wish to convey hurtful truths to a person on her deathbed, and sometimes happiness seems more important than knowledge.

Culver and Gert relate other cases of paternalism that involve other moral rule violations than depriving of freedom. However, they do not deny that there may be some limitation of freedom of action in these cases. They simply do not think that the main reason some of them are objectionable (or require justification) is that they limit freedom. In doing so, they appear to give autonomy a lesser value than Dworkin and Archard because they think that there are cases where the abridgement of autonomy is a lesser moral rule violation than, for instance, deception. In minimizing the importance of the limitation on autonomy, however, I think that they ignore some common intuitions about fatherly behavior. If we consider what typically makes fatherly behavior objectionable, it is not because fathers as a rule behave immorally, but because they (like mothers) are liable to be overprotective. In trying to prevent harm or to benefit their children, most fathers are prone to err not by breaking moral rules but by preventing a child from learning from the consequences of her mistakes. Fathers err in not allowing their children sufficient freedom to grow and to achieve independence. In the case of an adult who is treated paternalistically, the action is objectionable because such well-meant treatment limits her freedom to that of a child.

The advantage of accepting the view that paternalism always has negative connotations is that it makes easier to understand why any paternalistic act needs to be justified or held to close moral scrutiny. Kultgen prefers that the philosophical definition be value neutral although he agrees that the technical term is always at least mildly pejorative (61, 63). In the medical cases that Culver and Gert are specifically concerned with in their discussion of paternalism, it is clearly important that no paternalistic act escape this scrutiny. For their purposes, a *prima facie* requirement of moral justification is essential because medical professionals should always be held to account for their paternalistic actions. It can be argued that in any case in which the state interferes with its citizens' lives, a moral justification is needed as well.

From the foregoing, Dworkin's three conditions for paternalism appear to be defensible in terms of its capacity to answer objections and counterexamples. Restated, the definition is P acts paternalistically toward Q if and only if (a) P acts with the intent of averting some harm or promoting some benefit for Q; (b) P acts contrary to (or is indifferent to) the current preferences, desires, or values of Q; and (c) P's act is a limitation on Q's autonomy or liberty.

While it is possibly correct to consider this type of action more broadly, I believe that Dworkin's definition is useful for my purposes because it draws attention to the rationality of the subject acted on and to concerns about justifying the limitation to his autonomy that the act requires. For Dworkin, the subject is an autonomous being who has values, choices, and desires. She is not only capable of being benefited but is capable of choosing or refusing this benefit. According to my account of punishment, those we punish have the same capacities in regard to moral education. We do not require a broader conception.

JUSTIFYING PATERNALISTIC ACTS

I have argued that moral education is a necessary part of the justification of punishment. It is also important to understand how morally educating the persons we punish is itself justified. It is justified in the way in which any paternalistic act is justified with due consideration given to the well-being of the person who is acted on. In the philosophical literature, different conceptions are suggested as to what this well-being requires from either a deontological or a consequentialist normative standard. These standards sometimes vary from each other in terms of focusing on either minimizing evils or maximizing goods. In any case, however, consideration for the well-being of persons seems to minimally entail valuing their rational capacities and their ability to choose and to appreciate what is good or evil for themselves. Furthermore, there are varying conceptions of the value of autonomy in relation to other goods, and there are different perceptions of when a person's autonomy may be infringed by acting in her behalf.

One example of a deontological justification is provided by Culver and Gert.[1] They claim that to justify a paternalistic action, we must take into account (1) the moral rules which are violated; (2) the probable amount of evil caused, avoided, or ameliorated by the moral rule violation; and (3) the rational desires of the person(s) affected by the moral rule violation (148). In their view, moral rules may only be violated if greater evil can be prevented than is caused by violating the rule. The probable amount of evil includes the kind and severity of the evil, and the probable length of time it will be suffered. They define rational desires as either that which it would be irrational not to desire (the rationally required desires) or that which it would not be irrational not to desire (the rationally allowed desires). A simple example of a rationally required desire would be a desire to live when one's life is going well, and an example of a rationally allowed desire would be the desire for ice cream when one has the appetite for it and means of getting it. Rationality is here defined in terms of irrationality, so they avoid classifying purely impulsive acts as irrational. An irrational desire is the desire to harm oneself without adequate reason. Having an adequate reason for desiring to suffer harm means that one has weighed the evils that oneself or others will experience if one does not experience the harm and believes it to be weightier than the harm (Culver and Gert, 21; 26-27; 29-31; 148).

This conception seems to fit nicely with evaluating cases of medical paternalism, where it does not seem justified for doctors to interfere with their patients' lives without consent unless the patient truly has no adequate reason for refusing to be interfered with. Typically, doctors have no reason to paternalistically intervene unless the patient's choices are impaired by mental illness. Culver and Gert observe that the standard accounts of rationality (those endorsed by Hume and Rawls) are unable to classify the irrational desires of severely impaired mentally ill persons. Their account of rationality allows doctors to consider the choices of those individuals irrational and thus justifiably ignored when it will be to their benefit.

It is less certain, however, that this justification can be extended elsewhere. First, Culver and Gert's conception of rationality leaves no room for nonrational desire, or desires that are neither rational nor irrational. They claim that impulsive actions done without a reason, such as impulsively picking a flower, fall into the class of rational actions, but this broad conception would make animal behavior rational as well. As they deny that we can behave paternalistically toward animals, their conception of rationality seems too broad. Second, in their description of adequate reasons as "a balancing act of evils" one may still wonder how one can clearly evaluate how well this balancing act has been achieved. One may wonder how a rational person would weigh conflicting evils without any substantive conception of what humans or individuals need. While they try to express their intuitions regarding the proper weights of different evils by presenting various real-life examples, their justification may ultimately be circular.

Another deontological normative standard comes from Dworkin and Danny Scoccia. It is deontological in that it is based on a right not to be interfered with except when certain conditions are met. In an early paper, Dworkin says that paternalistic actions are justified if the person acted on would consent if she were well informed and fully rational (Dworkin 1983a, 28). Kultgen has presented a convincing attack on this conception of the justification of paternalism as based on the consent of an imaginary rational person. Kultgen says the imaginary rational person has nothing to do with the person acted on, and his consent can thus mean nothing to her. It is only the person's actual rationality that has value for her and not any imaginary rationality. As Kultgen remarks, the rational judge is simply the parentalist trying to be rational. In trying to be rational, the parentalist imposes his own standards of rationality (Kultgen, 123).

A similar objection can be found in the view that Scoccia attributes to Feinberg, Glover, Van de Veer, and Arneson, who believe that choices can be voluntary without being fully rational. Feinberg and these others believe that a person's autonomy is always violated when we interfere with a voluntary but irrational choice for the chooser's own good. They hold that philosophers such as Dworkin would wrongly tolerate the thwarting of impetuous and imprudent choices, such as one a person with a bohemian or adventurous lifestyle might choose. Scoccia responds to this objection with another conception of rational choice. For Scoccia, a choice is rational if it is likely to maximize the satisfaction of one's desires. This formal definition of rationality will not rule out the impetuous choices of the bohemian. Culver and Gert, however, criticize this particular conception for also not ruling out the actions of mentally ill persons who desire to engage in self-destructive behavior (25) (Scoccia, 318-320).

While Scoccia does not directly address the objection from Culver and Gert, he responds to a related objection by placing a caveat on the value of rational choice. He says that preferences or values may be less than fully autonomous. Since some people have nonautonomous desires (desires produced by behavioral conditioning or chemical injections) and some people have low autonomy desires (desires created, for example, by a neurosis or childhood peers), not all desires have equal worth. He describes highly autonomous desires (those that are most valuable) as desires that have survived some process of critical scrutiny and that mesh with their possessor's temperament, character, talents, and proclivities. He says a highly autonomous chooser will have deliberated at length about her values, and she will have a harmonious, coherent, and unique personality. (She will, thus, by implication not be subject to mental illness.) He finds substantive value in having highly autonomous desires. Consequently, he justifies paternalistic intervention if (a) "the person has highly autonomous desires, but the choice does not accurately express those desires and the person would consent to the interference if he were fully rational" [as in Mill's case of the person about to walk on the dangerous bridge]; (b) "the person has low autonomy desires" [as in the case of a child or adolescent], "he lacks the capacity to form highly autonomous desires, and the interference is necessary to preserve his potential to develop it later"; or (c) "the person has low autonomy desires" [as in the case of a neurotic individual], "the interference would increase the autonomy of his desires" (e.g., by removing an obstacle like neurosis or false consciousness to autonomous desire formation), and "the person would not object to the interference if he were rational and had high autonomy desires" (330-331). In every justifiable case, Scoccia justifies interference that promotes and develops autonomy. In the case where the person has highly autonomous desires, intervention without consent is only allowed because he is not fully rational, which for Scoccia seems to mean only that he lacks full information about what will happen to him. (If I am correct about his limited conception of full rationality, Scoccia may well be able to meet Kultgen's objection to ideal consent. No one else's rational standards would then be imposed on the highly autonomous person.) In Scoccia's view, autonomy is the greatest good for any individual, but not just any sort of autonomy. Rather, the greatest good is found in the autonomy that reflects a certain well-balanced and unique personality.

In contrast with Scoccia, Kultgen states that autonomy is not the greatest good, but is only one good among others. There is some evidence that Dworkin agrees with Kultgen here, particularly when Dworkin states that it need not be irrational to want to be a slave (Dworkin 1983b, 111). In Culver and Gert's discussion of a balancing of evils, it appears that they also doubt that autonomy is always the supreme good. Nevertheless, I think that there is some reason to believe that Kultgen and the others ultimately share many of the same values with Scoccia.

Kultgen bases his justification of parentalistic acts on a "reasonable" or moderate consequentialist standard. He says that consequentialists recognize that parentalists may benefit persons they act on in terms of life, health, and moral development, and these goods can outweigh the sacrifice of autonomy and "pride of self." For Kultgen, the greatest good is to be involved in caring relationships. He thinks that the caring person is most concerned with the effect of her efforts on the objective well-being of those for whom she cares, and thus she must be a consequentialist. However, he refers to his view as a "reasonable" consequentialism, because he recognizes the possibility of harm without strict limitations on parentalistic acts (Kultgen, 75-76). Kultgen formulates his justification of parentalism on the following consequentialist grounds. He says that persons are justified in acting parentalistically if and only if they believe that the expected value of the action for the recipient is greater than any alternative and they have reason to trust their own judgment despite the opposition of anyone, including the recipient (76).

Note that there is no explicit reference to autonomy in this justification, and it allows for the possibility that the recipient's consent (even ideal consent) can be completely disregarded. It is somewhat similar to Culver and Gert's balancing of evils, which suggests that their "reasonable" deontological position and this reasonable consequentialist position may closely mesh. However, I think it is superior to Culver and Gert's in its focus on a positive standard. While they provide a merely negative standard in their focus on minimizing evils, Kultgen's positive account can weigh goods on the basis of which goods will enhance survival and well-being both presently and in the future. A purely negative account, on the other hand, cannot as readily determine which outcomes are the most damaging because it lacks a clear conception of basic need.

On the other hand, Kultgen's justification of paternalistic acts need not be considered completely at odds with those who think of autonomy as the highest value because he also claims that autonomy is a great good. While Kultgen values caring as the greatest good, he also endorses Fromm's view of the ideal maternal and paternal love. Ideal parental love is always interested in fostering growth and independence. Independence is essential to survival and living well. Thus, in his corollaries to his justification Kultgen indicates certain necessary implications (77):

1. A person contemplating intervention in another person's life should seek consent, if possible.
2. When a subject's disabilities or encumbrances justify intervention, the intervention should extend only to the affected areas.
3. The encroachment on autonomy should be held to a minimum, even at a sacrifice of some of the benefits she is attempting to provide.
4. If possible, the parentalist should act to enhance the subject's future autonomy, terminating the parentalist relationship as soon as the subject is capable of self-care.
5. The parentalist should take into consideration the effect of the act on her own habits and the practices of others.
6. The parentalist should remain open to help from others when it is needed.

Clearly, in these corollaries respect for the autonomy of the subject acted on and an interest in fostering that autonomy, wherever possible, are important side constraints on any parentalistic act. Autonomy is important to Kultgen, though he claims that it is not the supreme good. He does not think autonomy is a supreme good because he questions the value of many choices persons make. He doubts that there is anything inherently valuable in making foolish or damaging choices. Autonomy is only a good insofar as it enhances our capacity for living well.

The essential difference between philosophers such as Kultgen and Scoccia in their valuation of autonomy may be reminiscent of the difference between Socrates and Aristotle in their valuation of virtue. Socrates (and probably Plato as well) famously claims that virtue is knowledge, while Aristotle denies the identity relation and maintains instead that virtue (i.e., full virtue) entails knowledge. Aristotle makes a distinction in having the natural virtues and being fully virtuous and between simple cleverness and practical wisdom that Socrates does not. These distinctions help Aristotle explain how moral education requires the help of practical wisdom. Like Aristotle, Kultgen claims that caring is not identical with an interest in promoting autonomy but merely entails that interest. A caring parent, in Kultgen's view, will promote autonomy not for its own sake but for the other benefits it provides to her growing child. Autonomy allows her to survive and to develop competence in many areas that can serve her needs and that of others.

Scoccia, on the other hand, may be regarded as fitting the Socratic mold in endorsing the view that the good parent always promotes autonomy for its own sake in her child. However, he is actually more consistent with Aristotle and Kultgen because of the distinction he draws between desires which are highly autonomous and those which are not. Desires which are highly autonomous have survived critical scrutiny and mesh with the person's unique temperament, character, talents, and proclivities. The values represented by the objects of these desires have been tested by consideration of rival values. Using an example from Scoccia, "the autonomous ascetic has worked out his opinions about the advantages and disadvantages of the voluptuary's life" (328). On the other hand, desires which have low autonomy are only the product of social conditioning, most of which will not be fitted to an individual's particular nature. It is expected that persons such as children, adolescents, and the mentally impaired will be less capable of having highly autonomous desires because they are impeded in some way (e.g., by youth or neurosis) in testing the desires and values they have been conditioned to have. Hence, Scoccia can readily explain the greater need for paternalistic action in regards to these individuals.

Kultgen and Scoccia are consistent in providing a developmental understanding of autonomy. For both, there are important qualitative differences in forms of autonomy, and the lower forms of autonomy do not particularly deserve respect. They also concur in respecting and valuing the highest form of autonomy, and they respect it for what it means for the person who has it. They differ, however, about whether to rate it as the sole substantive value for justified paternalism.

In my opinion, paternalistic acts are justified only when they both maximize benefits to the persons who are acted on and do not interfere with those persons' well-informed highly autonomous desires. Kultgen and Scoccia provide these two necessary conditions for justifying paternalistic acts. Considered together, their justifications may well be sufficient. Kultgen's justification alone is insufficient because it does not require that paternalistic acts support highly autonomous desires. His justification, in spite of his corollaries, allows for the possibility that I could prevent my adult son from taking part in a dangerous sport, which he loves and is quite skilled at, because of my fears of the danger to him. In loving my son, I naturally wish to maximize his life expectancy. If I firmly believe that he is endangering his life by engaging in this sport, I will be justified according to Kultgen in preventing him from exercising his highly autonomous desire. I am not, however, justified in doing so. It is possible that I am misinformed about the risks to my son, whose skill at this sport may minimize the dangers, and I do not understand that the main way for him to express his talents is to engage in this sport.

I think that it is likely that Scoccia will agree with me about this case, assuming that Scoccia only means by being fully rational having full information. If, for example, my son were not fully aware of the risks he was taking in practicing this sport, I would have good reason to intervene. Conversely, if he were fully aware of the risks, I most likely would not. Scoccia says that it is uncertain (and probably doubtful) whether being rational means being prudent or cautious about taking dangerous risks. We do not want to call the martyr for a glorious cause, the terminally ill patient who wishes to die or the person who thrives on thrill-seeking adventures irrational. Each of those persons has his or her own ideas about his or her well-being. If we mean to respect what is truly good for them, then we need to be very careful not to impose our own notions of living well on them.

On the other hand, if we consider the case of my thrill-seeking son, we can also find a counterexample to Scoccia's justification. Suppose that my son is fully informed about the risk of his sport, and he means to practice it in a manner that he knows has a very high probability of ending in his death. The likely prospect of death does not daunt him because he thinks the thrill will be worth it. From Scoccia's account, I cannot interfere with his choice because it accurately expresses his highly autonomous desires. However, if I do not interfere he will surely die, and he will no longer be able to engage in this sport or in any other fulfilling activity. Further, if he has any regard for his family or other loved ones, he will be depriving himself of any further contact with them.

Consequently, Scoccia's justification of paternalistic behavior is limited and possibly somewhat selfish in outcome in cases of the type just mentioned. In its sole focus on individual goods, it does not consider the goods we have simply by virtue of being human. Kultgen's account, however, does respect these other human values, and particularly the value of being involved in a caring relationship.

I recognize, of course, at this juncture that both Kultgen and Scoccia may claim that I misunderstand their intent. It may in fact be the case that their justifications are ultimately equivalent. For instance, if Kultgen's parentalist really has a good reason for intervening, it may be that she knows the truth about what the subject needs in terms of the subject's individual values and human values. If Scoccia means that to have a personality that is harmonious and coherent means that one is not only not mentally impaired but also emotionally well-adjusted, then it may also include desires for such human goods as mutually caring relationships.

A justified paternalistic act should take into account both individual and human needs. It should account for our need to express our unique talents, but it should also account for our need to express our human talents. Possibly the most important human talent is the talent to be involved in mutually caring relationships with others. A justified paternalism finds worth in being a person who can fully express his individual talents and who can also fully express his specifically human talents.

Consequently, I believe that a paternalistic act is justified if and only if (a) the person so acting believes that the expected value of the action for the recipient in terms of the recipient's human and individual needs is greater than any alternative and she has reason to trust her own judgment despite the opposition of anyone, including the recipient; and (b) the recipient has low autonomy desires or the recipient has highly autonomous desires and would consent if she were fully informed about the consequences of intervention. Note that these two criteria are a minor abridgment of Kultgen's and Scoccia's standards. In the former case I want the paternalist to be mindful of human well-being and to be mindful of the particular needs and character of the unique individual she wishes to benefit. In the latter case I recognize that intervention with persons whose choices reflect only low autonomy desires may need assistance even if they are incapable of developing highly autonomous desires in the future. Intervention should, however, aim to promote autonomy whenever possible.

JUSTIFYING STATE PATERNALISM IN PUNISHING

The form of state paternalism that I advocate has the advantage of being only thinly paternalistic. The benefit to be accrued through being justifiably punished is merely the opportunity to acquire the mandatory moral virtues (in Pincoffs' terms) or the sort of character that will not use immoral means (in Prust's terms). To be justified, punishment does not have to make persons acquire moral ends, though acquiring those ends would be a greater benefit. In this section, I provide a justification for this thin form of state paternalism by the following. First, I measure it in terms of the criteria just given for justifying any paternalistic act. Second, I consider how it holds up to Kultgen's four criteria for justifiable state paternalism. Third, I argue that it is a defensible form of legal moralism along the lines of Kultgen's conception and possibly a defensible legal perfectionism in spite of the worries of liberals such as Joel Feinberg.

I have claimed that to educate a person morally by means of punishment is a form of state paternalism because moral education is intended to be a benefit. If one has the mandatory moral virtues in the sense that one avoids harming others, then one is less likely to be socially isolated and shunned. Being shunned is an evil to persons because it diminishes self-respect and makes it difficult to pursue individual projects.

Using the first standard, punishment for the purpose of moral education must have a greater value for the recipient than any alternative. The alternatives for the state in dealing with an offender are to not punish at all or to punish only for the purpose of benefiting others (e.g., by the self-protection or deterrence accounts). The second alternative has no value for the recipient and is not paternalistic. The first alternative may appear to the happy psychopath like the best alternative, but it is in fact the worst. To not punish is to inform the offender that the state and society see nothing culpable in his offending, and it would probably encourage him to continue offending, and probably in a worse manner. By continued offending, he will become increasingly isolated, antisocial, and narcissistic as his sense of entitlement to commit whatever offenses he likes grows. Thus, punishing in order to educate the person morally meets the first standard for justified paternalism.

Assessing the paternalism of punishment by the second standard, it is doubtful that the criminal offender who is justly punished could be regarded as having highly autonomous desires which reflect his unique temperament, character, talents, and proclivities. The values expressed in desires to commit criminal offenses are not likely to have been carefully deliberated, nor do they seem unique to any individual. For example, the desire to commit violent offenses is often produced in violent family or community backgrounds. Desires to steal may result from a narcissistic sense of entitlement (which is in no way unique and need not reflect a person's actual talents) or by the influence of criminal peers. It seems probable that the desire to commit criminal offenses is not a highly autonomous desire. Consequently, this type of state paternalism is justified by the second standard.

It is also justified by means of Scoccia's more narrow standard. Recall that Scoccia says that low autonomy desires may be interfered with when either the person lacks the capacity to form highly autonomous desires, and the interference is necessary to preserve his potential to develop it later, or the interference would increase the autonomy of his present desires and he would not object if he were rational and had high autonomy desires. The first class of low autonomy desires seems to apply chiefly to youths who are quite susceptible to peer pressure. In that many offenders are emotionally immature for their age, some fall into this class. The second class seems to include persons who have low autonomy desires due to some sort of mental disorder, which impedes though does not completely eliminate their rational capacities. Many, though not all, offenders are impaired by a mental disorder that causes them to act impulsively and thoughtlessly. Since persons who are justly punished have the capacity for prudential rationality and have reasonable alternatives to their offenses, I believe that they can all be described as either immature or having a mental disorder. Given that their emotional immaturity or mental disorder limits their autonomy, the paternalistic intervention of punishment is warranted. In either case, it is warranted if the intervention will improve their capacity for having highly autonomous desires in the future. The moral education of punishment, if successful, is intended to meet the goal of increasing the level of autonomy of these offenders. It can meet this goal because higher levels of autonomy reflect improvements in moral behavior.

It can be objected, of course, that there are important differences between acts of paternalism by individuals and by large corporate bodies, such as states. State paternalism of punishment may require further or even different justification than individual. Kultgen has examined these differences. He says that states generally act paternalistically toward classes of individuals who have common needs, and the state is not likely to fully comprehend individual needs as well as the individual paternalist. It tends to act in an impersonal manner because many different state officials are involved in legislating and enforcing public goods. In the process, state paternalism is at great risk for losing sight of the benefits to the recipients. Consequently, Kultgen says, in any case of state paternalism it is particularly imperative for agents of the state to have accurate knowledge that the benefit to the recipient will be secured and that the action of the state is truly the best alternative for her. To minimize the risk, Kultgen offers four useful standards for judging acts of state paternalism. These are standards that appear to be appropriately applied as additions to the basic justification of individual acts of paternalism. They do not supplant the original justification of any paternalistic act. Rather, they function as codicils for this particular type of paternalism (Kultgen, 161-162).

Firstly, Kulten says that "people acting for a corporate group should restrict their efforts to basic needs that can be served by manipulating external conditions" (162). With this standard, the state, for instance, may be permitted to heavily tax tobacco products and alcohol while not prohibiting their use. The basic need in this instance is health. Taxation would not eliminate the choice to use these drugs, though it may limit it in some cases. In regards to punishment, I have argued that persons have a basic need to take only moral means toward their ends. By means of justified punishment, the state alters the present environment of offenders with the intention of encouraging them to change their external behavior. The state does not rightfully do this by any form of conditioning to alter their moral ends. Rather, the state must respect the individual's moral autonomy in punishing and must leave it to the offender to determine his own ends. Thus, as I interpret it, moral education by means of punishing meets this standard.

Kultgen's second standard is that the state, in acting paternalistically, must regard the autonomy of the recipient as an important good, though at times not as important as the particular good, such as health or security, which is the state's specific responsibility (162). For instance, martial law may seem beneficial to a riot-torn community, but the benefit may be questionable when the law prevents citizens from engaging in any of their normal occupations. In the case of justified punishment, I have argued that the autonomy of the offender is always respected. Justified punishment, in fact, will promote the possibility that the offender will become increasingly autonomous as he learns and appreciates its moral message.

Kultgen's third standard is that the state should encourage the development of institutions that will share burdens with it, and the state should itself act at the lowest, most local or personal level at which it can be effective (162). This standard speaks to appropriate limits on state paternalism, and these limits are well applied to punishment by the state. It would certainly be preferable if the state did not need to punish at all for its citizens to be morally educated. If parents, schools, and other local community organizations did an adequate job of preparing the youth to enter the world by fostering and promoting moral behavior, it seems likely that state punishment would not be needed. In any event, the moral education of punishment is and should be the last resort for the morally incorrigible offender, subsequent to other more local measures. When punishment must occur, I think this standard continues to hold. For instance, in a prison environment moral education is more likely to be successful if the staff-to-inmate ratio is sufficiently small so that the rehabilitation needs of inmates can be understood and addressed. Prison staff are more likely to understand the needs of their inmates when the numbers are manageable.

Kultgen's fourth standard is that the state should utilize measures that encourage and equip individuals to tend to their own needs whenever possible (162). This standard indicates that the state should always try to promote independence. Clearly, the state is acting in a self-defeating manner if in punishing it promotes the dependency of institutionalization or recidivism. Sometimes these consequences occur as a result of punishment. If they do, then punishment has failed. Of course, any benevolent action has the potential for failure, and its justification partially rests on minimizing that risk. Punishment which is justified will aim to minimize that risk as well. I have argued that punishment as a tool of moral education can benefit offenders by giving them reason to eschew immoral means. In eschewing immoral means, these offenders become more autonomous beings. They are freed from the urge to act on those desires that will place them at risk for being punished again and that will effectively serve to alienate them from others who can help them grow and prosper. Therefore, justified punishment by the state aims to promote independence and also aims to minimize the possibility of the cure being worse to the patient than the disease.

Taken together, these four standards emphasize that the state must respect and promote the autonomy of those it means to benefit and that the state must be aware of and try to compensate for its inevitable psychological distance from those persons. Kultgen believes that the state is most likely to err if it does not meet these standards. While the standards may not be exhaustive, they appear to adequately address the particular character of the state as a paternalistic agent.

From the foregoing, it appears that moral education by means of punishment is a defensible form of state paternalism in its ability to meet the proposed standards for justified paternalism and state paternalism. However, another objection remains which pertains to the defensibility of any form of state paternalism. Paternalism by the state is sometimes objected to as a form of legal moralism or legal perfectionism.

Legal moralism is the view that law may properly be used to enforce morality. Its most notable adherent was Lord Patrick Devlin, and it is a view of law that has been roundly criticized. One criticism is that legal moralism will enforce conventional morality for its own sake independently of whether the prohibited behavior harms others or the agent herself. Kultgen has responded to this criticism by first claiming that legal moralism is non-parentalistic. Parentalistic acts are concerned with what will truly benefit the person acted on. A purely conventional morality, which condemns certain forms of behavior, may not promote what is truly in the best interest of those it is imposed on. Second, he claims that the moral life of citizens is a legitimate concern of the state because its raison d'être is the good life for its members and moral action is essential to the good life. Kultgen advocates an indirect legal moralism because the state is very limited in its capacities to promote the truly moral life. Thus, he says the state should rarely try to enforce strict rules of behavior, which Devlin has been criticized for recommending. Rather, the state should "promote a hospitable environment" for schools, families, and other community groups which educate the youth in acquiring good values. The state should also encourage wide-ranging discussion and critical evaluations of moral beliefs among all of its citizens. Thus, it should encourage freedom of expression and conscience. In this way, the state is properly concerned with morally educating its citizens. By this means, it not only morally educates but also increases autonomy (Kultgen, 173-175).

I believe that my moral education account is consistent with Kultgen's conception of legal moralism. I have argued that, in enforcing certain just laws, the state means to promote the good of rational behavior. The state respects rationality when it only punishes those who can view punishment as a reason not to offend and when it intends to appeal to the offender's prudential rationality in punishing. Punishment is meant to give the offender a reason not to offend in the future. Justified punishment, of course, only pertains to offenses that are clearly harmful to others and are, unarguably, immoral actions. Thus, punishment on this account is not a form of legal moralism of the Devlin variety, because it does not justify punishing in order to morally educate those who only breach conventional morality or who only in some way harm themselves.

Some liberals, such as Feinberg, may claim that I am advocating a form of legal perfectionism when I only need the harm principle to justify punishment. In *Harmless Wrongdoing,* Feinberg says the principle of legal perfectionism is that "it is a proper aim of the criminal law to perfect the character and elevate the tastes of the citizens who are subject to it" (277). Legal perfectionists typically see the criminal law as a means to inculcate the moral virtues. Many philosophers who have endorsed moral education in the past can be described as legal perfectionists, particularly as they understand the principal function of the criminal law as a means of helping persons to acquire moral ends. I have rejected the view that punishment is meant for this purpose because I recognize its virtual impossibility in the cases of many persons we believe can be rightfully punished. Rather, I have indicated that justified punishment is intended to help persons eschew immoral means. If it does so, it can be said that punishment helps persons acquire the mandatory moral virtues (in Pincoffs' terms) or the sort of character that will no longer commit offenses (in Prust's terms). While I do not think the enforcement of the criminal law through punishment is likely in many cases to "perfect" offenders or even to improve their tastes (goals), I do think it can improve and benefit them. Thus, strictly speaking, my account does not fit Feinberg's description of legal perfectionism.

Feinberg acknowledges that a moral education account of the justification of punishment need not be inconsistent with liberalism when he discusses Hampton's account (300-305). In presenting her moral education theory, Hampton says moral education theory cannot answer the question of what should be made law or which ethical reasons warrant the imposition of a law. In making this claim, she differs from my account as I have argued that moral education can only take place by means of punishment of violations of just laws, which include laws that harm others. If there are not some laws that it is clearly immoral to violate, it seems questionable that a person can be truly educated about moral values by legal punishment.

Feinberg, in fact, points out a dilemma for any moral education account when it is dissociated from legal perfectionism (302). If the standards that are violated are purely conventional, then they are also arbitrary, and no reason can be forthcoming on why the standards exist. The state imposing only conventional standards can say that they exist to make the offender a better person, but it can give no further reason why violating the standards would make someone a worse person. Feinberg says the alternative is to say that the standards are there in order to prevent harm to others. The state could explain that it would make you a worse person to harm others, and it is the state's ideal that virtuous persons do not knowingly harm others. However, in that case, Feinberg says that the harm principle is the primary reason for the standard and the issue of enhancing virtue is merely derivative or secondary.

Clearly, I take the second horn of Feinberg's dilemma. However, I think his objection to the second horn can be answered. He does not take into account the value of being a person who does not take immoral means. Recall Rawls' argument that the virtues are excellences. Given that any rational person has unique talents that she wishes to exercise with increasing complexity and that she requires the assistance and support of others to enjoy the exercise of these talents, any rational person will be better off by not harming others. Certain offenders may, of course, have criminal talents which they enjoy exercising. Punishment by means of incarceration will most likely frustrate these talents, and punishment will at the same time frustrate the exercise of their noncriminal talents as well. For instance, safecrackers have mechanical aptitudes that could be noncriminally exercised. Even pickpockets have visual and manual talents that could be otherwise exercised. Should they not be apprehended, it is at least likely that their social relationships will be significantly impaired.

On the other hand, it can be objected that I am not advocating punishment as moral education but only punishment as prudential education. This objection, however, misunderstands the importance of prudence for morality. A person cannot be prudent for the benefit of others if she has not learned to be prudent for herself. To be a prudent person, one must be capable of rational reflection. One must be able to rationally weigh the benefits to oneself of different possible actions. Many offenders are quite impulsive and deficient in this rational capacity. They are imprudent as well as immoral. To be a moral person as well as a prudent one requires more complex rational reflection on the consequences of one's actions. It requires the capacity to make logical or imaginative inferences about how one would feel if she were in another's place and which of her actions she would find most beneficial if she were in the other's place. Thus, prudent action requires a minimal reflective capacity that is a necessary precondition to moral action. Prudence is a necessary first step in the process of moral development.

While it is true that many offenders do not seem capable of moving beyond this first step, it is still a step in the right direction.

Like many liberals, Feinberg places ultimate value on the autonomy of individuals so he is inclined to only endorse the self-protection or nonpaternalist justification of punishment. Nonetheless, as Kultgen has argued, even Feinberg expresses mixed beliefs regarding the value of consent for parentalistic acts in persons with varying degrees of competence and acknowledges the difficulties inherent in determining when consent becomes either perfectly voluntary or perfectly involuntary (Kultgen, 182-183). Thus, Feinberg is only "softly" anti-paternalistic. He seems to acknowledge that there are varying levels of autonomy in different persons and that these varying levels have different values. In the next chapter I will explore in more depth the various forms and values of autonomy that are found in offenders we punish and in offenders who have been morally educated or who have successfully completed correctional counseling.

NOTE

1. The descriptions of Culver and Gert's views in this chapter are taken from their 1982 book, *Philosophy in Medicine*. Their 1997 book, *Bioethics: A Return to Fundamentals*, presents some minor alterations of their conception of paternalism and its justification. However, the concerns here expressed remain relevant because their views are not substantially altered in revision.

Chapter Four

Self-Determination

To claim that an offender is morally culpable because his offense was freely committed while also claiming that a goal of correctional counseling is to help him become self-determining is to imply a developmental understanding of freedom or self-determination. In this chapter I will present a developmental conception that is designed to resolve the puzzle of how the offender can be both free and not free. In this discussion, I am using the terms self-determination, autonomy, and freedom interchangeably. While freedom may be construed more broadly than autonomy or self-determination, I stipulate here that a person is free or autonomous or self-determining in any given situation only if she is capable of finding reasons to act otherwise. I am excluding external senses of freedom such as being free to vote because one has reached the age of twenty-one or being free to purchase a fast car because one has the money. An external sense of freedom pertains only to the physical circumstances of the agent, and it does not require that she have some degree of rationality. Self-determination in my usage is an internal property of some individuals and entails a degree of rationality. It is a reason for holding persons morally culpable, and it is present in those who have the best and most moral life when it is most fully developed.

There are many alternative accounts in the philosophical literature of the basis for human freedom and moral responsibility. I think that one of the most plausible accounts is provided by Maurice Merleau-Ponty, who explains human freedom as "a meeting of the inner and outer" by arguing that humans are determined by the world and also determine their manner of being in the world. While Merleau-Ponty does not provide a full developmental account of freedom, his conception is consistent with that provided by Mitchell Aboulafia, who shows how self-determination develops out of the prereflective consciousness. Aboulafia has synthesized some of the insights of G. H. Mead and Jean-Paul Sartre to show how freedom comes to be through the development in consciousness of the object-self and the not-self. His conception, I believe, parallels the progress of moral development in an individual found in Lawrence Kohlberg's account of the moral stages. I will explain this parallel in order to show that the most autonomous person is also a moral one and that increases in autonomy reflect increases in morality. I will conclude by utilizing this explanation to resolve the previously mentioned puzzle.

MERLEAU-PONTY'S
CONCEPTION OF SELF-DETERMINATION

Merleau-Ponty argues that freedom can only be understood in the context of a historical subject. Persons cannot choose the world they find themselves in, but they can choose their manner of being in the world. He defends this claim in his chapter entitled "Freedom" in *Phenomenology of Perception* by showing that the claims of pure subjectivity and pure objectivity are wrong. Pure subjectivity can be regarded as complete indeterminism, the idea that human subjects are always free in their actions and passions and nothing determines what they will do or desire. This position asserts that meanings or significations only exist when they are imposed on the world by human subjects. For instance, the rock face of a cliff only becomes an obstacle if it is my project to climb it. However, Merleau-Ponty argues that if this were true, there would be no free action. For if we are not in some way specified by the world, then it is not possible for us to affect the world in our acting. (By specified, I take him to mean that the world makes of each of us a thing with certain natural and sociocultural properties.) He says that a subject must have being because nonbeing cannot pass into the being of the world. It must, therefore, be specified or determined by the world. Only in being specified is there a range of real possibilities. On the other hand, he claims that pure objectivity is also false. While I cannot choose the fact that at this moment I am fatigued, I am free to choose my feelings toward my fatigue. I can choose to like or dislike it.

Merleau-Ponty explains that freedom commences with a consciousness becoming aware of itself as part of a natural and cultural world, and it is through this world that it comes to understand itself. Humans are social and historical beings who exercise their freedom through committing themselves in a certain manner to the world they find themselves in. For example, the proletarian is a person in a certain socioeconomic situation who need not be conscious of his situation or define himself in those terms. It is only when this person has difficulty making ends meet, looks around and discovers others in the same predicament, and joins forces with those others to force a raise in wages that he sees himself as a proletarian and his situation becomes "revolutionary." The proletarian's freedom develops with his consciousness of having a certain form of being, recognizing that same being in others, and deciding to respond to having that being in a particular way. This form of freedom is contingent on the meanings or significations that the world and other persons similarly constituted impose on him because these meanings are the field from which he establishes the meanings and direction of his own life.

For Merleau-Ponty, meanings are imposed on us by our culture and socioeconomic situation through other persons, who are never merely objects to us but who are also free subjects. Merleau-Ponty says that individual existence requires this conception of intersubjectivity because "the-other-person-as-object is nothing but an insincere modality of others, just as absolute subjectivity is nothing but an abstract notion of myself" (448). If what I am, a "bourgeois" or a "man," is to have meaning, "I must apprehend myself immediately as centered in a way outside myself, and my individual existence must diffuse round itself, so to speak an existence in quality" (448). Thus, there must be significations imposed on us by others capable of doing so, and we must be capable as well of imposing our significations on those others. We are capable of doing this because the world is never completely constituted—there are always possibilities for changing the world and its significations. For Merleau-Ponty, the course of history is an exchange between generalized and individual existence, with each receiving and giving something. Freedom is, thus, a meeting of the inner and outer. We exist as both subjects and objects through recognizing and making commitments in regard to the meanings imposed on us.

While Merleau-Ponty's account is helpful in explaining how freedom develops through our awareness of the way in which the world acts on us and the way we respond to the meanings we find in the world, it is not fully explanatory of how freedom comes into being. Merleau-Ponty does not fully explain how the power of humans emerges, and he thus leaves in question whether freedom is a necessary feature of all humans. He also does not fully account for the importance of rational reflection and deliberation in the act of committing to a certain way of being in the world. Regardless of what his view may be, one may wonder if this commitment is entirely driven by the feelings of the agent. If this is the case, then it may be doubted that there is any rational basis for it.

These worries are not found in Aboulafia's developmental account of self-determination. Aboulafia is like Merleau-Ponty in emphasizing the importance of intersubjectivity in the development of freedom or, as he refers to it, mutual recognition, and in explaining this development as an exchange of meanings. He differs, however, in explaining this exchange of meanings via role-playing and in emphasizing the importance of rational reflection.

ABOULAFIA'S CONCEPTION
OF SELF-DETERMINATION[1]

According to Aboulafia's account, for a person to be self-determining, she must first develop a sense of self, which requires the internalization of negation. Aboulafia borrows this notion of a sense of self from Sartre, yet it takes on a different meaning in Aboulafia's analysis because in his view it cannot develop without the previous development of an object-self. The conception of an object-self he takes from Mead. The object-self is the self-as-object, and it can only be known by assuming the perspective of the other. For Mead, the other's perspective can only be assumed through taking her role (role playing), and doing so clearly requires linguistic abilities, which infants lack.

It seems uncontroversial to assert that infants are not free beings but have the potential to become free. The recent infant research (see Beebe, Lachmann, and Jaffe, 1997) has suggested that infants have some self-regulatory capacities as shown by evidence of cognitive organization of experience. However, in lacking the capacity for more abstract symbolic representations, infants clearly lack any conceptual sense of what they are or of the roles others play in relating to them. Therefore, they lack a sense of self, in Aboulafia's terms, which would give them a basis for choosing between alternatives and from which they can begin to become self-determining. Gaining a sense of self, according to his analysis, requires the ability to organize one's experience of the world symbolically and the ability to understand how one is qualitatively differentiated from it.

While Aboulafia does not precisely chart the development of the self-determining self in *The Mediating Self*, his description of this development suggests that a person essentially progresses through three stages of consciousness before realizing the final stage in which she is self-determined. These stages are: (1) the prereflective consciousness; (2) the prereflective sense of self; and (3) the reflective sense of self. Each later stage requires completion of the prior stage. Progress through the stages is not inevitable, but is contingent on physical and psychological health and the right sort of social environment.

Aboulafia agrees with Freud that at its earliest stage the human infant is in a stage of primary narcissism. In this stage, there is no differentiation between self and other or between self and world. However, the infant has many natural impulses and desires and begins to learn about the world when its impulses are thwarted. For example, it is denied breast or bottle when it is hungry. This denial is its first experience with prohibition. The prereflective consciousness begins to develop as feelings of conflict first emerge from feeling the impulse and the "no" of the other at the same time. (Initially, this consciousness is only consciousness of a negative feeling because it has not yet developed the cognitive self-as-object.) To resolve the conflict, the child must either internalize the prohibition through role playing (taking the role of the other and saying no to itself) or refuse the "no." This is the first situation the child encounters where alternatives exist.

The second choice is a poor one. Aboulafia says that refusing the "no" leaves the child in a paradox. Since being can only be defined by nonbeing, in refusing the "no" the child refuses its own being. In other words, the child is attempting to deny that which gives it its first sense of being as an object-self. It thus denies its very existence. It tries to negate that which gives it its first experience of negation, but it has already been defined through the negation of the other, and it can only say no because it has experienced this negation. The paradox of self-affirmation by means of self-negation is made clearer by Mead (Aboulafia, 79). For Mead, tactile experience alone will not show a child that things are embodied. To be embodied means that one has an inside as well as an outside. The child initially learns that things have insides by encountering resistance in things. To understand this resistance, the child must "take on both roles." It must take on the role of the thing that is resisting and it must take on the role of responding to the resistance. Only by doing so can the child begin to have a sense of his own embodiment. So, even having a body is mediated by our social experience. My body is mine because I have viewed it from the perspective of the other and internalized this perspective.

Aboulafia makes clear at this early stage that humans alone are capable of developing this prereflective consciousness. Some animals, like humans, have a sense of what they are not, which gives them some definition, but they lack awareness of the qualitative limits that internalizing the roles of others gives the developing person. To explain qualitative limits, he refers to Hegel's conception of limit, which pertains to determining a thing entirely by what it is not. Social experience provides humans the opportunity to encounter persons occupying many diverse roles, and these roles reflect differences in kind and a greater sense of what a person is not. On the other hand, nonhuman animals have no comprehension of this sort of social experience in that they are unable to view themselves from the role of the other. Consequently, when encountering prohibitions, animals only slink back. The development of empathy through role playing is a uniquely human trait.

In the prereflective consciousness, the object-self emerges as the child begins to internalize the perspective of others. The object-self grows as her social environment expands, and she internalizes the perspectives of new others that she encounters. But subjectivity does not emerge with only a developing object-self, even one that has developed a "generalized other" in Mead's terms. Rather, it only begins to emerge in the next stage as the prereflective sense of self comes into being through negation. Aboulafia defines this stage as "the noncognitively lived consciousness that has learned to live in sociality, between what it has been and the non-being of the future" (85). The object-self that has arisen in the pre-reflective consciousness develops not only by internalizing the responses of others, but also by practice with not accepting specific demands of others, through use of the "no." The toddler who repeatedly says "no" is acquiring a sense of self on a prereflective level, because these "nos" serve to differentiate himself from the other and enable him to begin to see himself as a being who is capable of inhibiting the other. These "nos" occur because novelty or the unexpected has entered the person's consciousness. (By novelty, I think that Aboulafia means new roles or new ways of playing old roles.) Novelty forces the evolving object-self that has learned to live in sociality to live between its object-self and that which it is not. As the person begins to discover that others are not completely predictable and to learn to expect the unexpected, she begins to see the world as a world of possibility. The ability to anticipate both the expected and the unexpected plays a critical role in developing the sense of self. Only through anticipating the unexpected does one come to be aware of a limit to consciousness through awareness of what one is not (i.e., most broadly, what one is not now nor has been, but can only be in the future).

In the next stage of consciousness, reflection transforms the awareness of the self. It transforms it and the awareness of what one lacks into "my" self and "my" lack. Aboulafia says that it is no accident that the child refers to herself in the third person before she can say and experience her own sense of self. When she begins to reflect, she begins to comprehend a dualism of subject and object. The prereflective sense of self, on the other hand, "lives in the quasi-unity of a stream of consciousness open to the future" (Aboulafia, 99). This means that the prereflective sense of self does not fully differentiate what she is now from what she may be in the future. Children go through a stage of confusing reality and fantasy, and in doing so, they seem to be expressing this prereflective sense of self.

With reflection comes an awareness of "I-ness," and Aboulafia refers to the reflective self that emerges as a "me-system." As the object-self develops in the "me-system," the novel is integrated into the old me-system, while the system reorganizes itself due to the presence of the novel element. The object-self is a relational and open system, living in sociality, and sociality allows and requires frequent alterations of the self. It is essentially altered by the novel it integrates into consciousness. Not every novel element is integrated, however, because the novel element must not be too different from the old system for it to be incorporated. A possible example of this phenomenon at an adult level may include awareness of the possibility of mountain climbing, but the psychological and physical requisites of being a mountain climber may be too foreign to the old "me-system" for that possibility to be accepted as one's own.

At the final stage, the person becomes self-determining, which Aboulafia describes as "the capacity to adjust a limit of the self by negating the not-self, so as to convert that which is other or imperfectly self into self, and it depends on the internalization of the no" (100). Reflection allows the person to consider what will and will not mesh with his old self, and which new elements will be most conducive to his functioning and development. Through greater knowledge and experience, the person is better able to identify which new elements will benefit him. A self-determining individual is capable of reflectively organizing the elements of his evolving "me-system."

Self-determination, however, not only requires reflective organization but also mutual recognition. That is, to be self-determining, we must recognize self-determination in others who recognize it in us. This is because the self does not develop in isolation; it always develops in sociality. Aboulafia depicts how self-determination finally emerges by referring to Hegel's story of the Master and Slave, which he finds somewhat analogous to the development of freedom in the child. Hegel's story is about the birth of self-consciousness, and it commences with two conscious beings who first become aware of each other by means of The Look, in which each becomes objectified in the eyes of the other. The two fight a battle to the death to resist becoming objectified, and the winner, who least fears death, becomes the Master and the loser the Slave.

Aboulafia relates that in the earliest days of the child's primitive object-self, the world first intrudes in the form of prohibitions by the other. In order to overcome this otherness or to reject becoming objectified, the child begins to make use of the verbal gesture no. In repeatedly saying no, he battles (like Hegel's Slave) to preserve himself as a whole being, and it is a battle that he (like the Slave) must eventually lose. He must lose the battle because his survival depends on it. He capitulates in order to live, and consequently makes the other into the object-self, which means that he has internalized and accepted the other's perspective of himself as an object. This object-self is not yet, however, his own, and he remains a mere thing like the Slave. The negative thus remains external to the child. He views himself entirely in terms of his role and the prohibitions he has accepted.

In Hegels' story, the Slave is first rescued by work. For the child as well, it is in his increasing power over things, in doing and mastering new tasks that he first experiences successful negation. Work alone, however, will not make the child free any more than the Slave is freed by his work. The child must also be recognized as a person who masters and executes tasks, who has the power of converting nonbeing into being. For the Slave, no such recognition from others is possible, but for the child, there is the possibility of real recognition. While the parent-child relationship is by definition hierarchical like the Master-Slave, the parent can recognize specific qualities, characteristics, behaviors, and roles of the child because the parent also possesses the roles and behaviors for which the child is recognized. For example, the parent can recognize parenting behavior when the child takes care of a doll. While the parent's recognition of the child's mastery is only simple in that it is limited to recognizing the other for mastering certain behaviors and roles, it paves the way for mutual recognition to occur in the future. In mutual recognition, one sees a person as having a future of his own, yet as being like oneself in also having a sense of self. The parent who believes that the child can and should be self-determining is interested in recognizing actions of the child that are conducive to independence and expects that in the future the parent and child will meet nonhierarchically and in mutual recognition.

Aboulafia makes clear that not all persons reach the stage of self-determination. To become self-determining a person must be recognized by others as capable of autonomy. Others must respond to her as a person and worthy of respect. In societies where there are not a sufficient number of roles and novel behaviors to learn, the self remains circumscribed, like that of the Slave. In certain societies, persons are not encouraged to become fully autonomous or to grow beyond the objectivity and dependency that those placed above them prefer them to remain in. Dependency is maintained when the other refuses to accept the child's no and does not provide a world for the child to affect and shape. Only if the child's no is accepted can its object-self be transformed into a sense of self.

Aboulafia's account as summarized here encapsulates the view of Merleau-Ponty and improves it by showing that cognitive advances in resolving internal contradictions within consciousness are the means by which self-determination becomes possible. These contradictions create conflictual feelings that are eventually resolved through rational reflection to determine the sort of self a person means to be and the sort of ends her self will value. Here we find rationally determined ends, but reason is not their sole determinant. Personal ends are also shaped by the developed object-self and the not-self. Contrary to the thesis of determinism, personal ends are not completely determined by the past. They are determined by the future as well—what she is not now but what she may come to be. The self-determined self correctly sees herself as living in a world of probability and not strictly determined by the object-self that she has previously been, while she also understands the limits of her "me-system." She discovers the significations the world imposes on her through her role-playing, and she makes her own significations on the world through her work and the intersubjective process of mutual recognition. She is both a subject and an object that lives in sociality.

KOHLBERG'S MORAL STAGES[2]

In mutual recognition I see myself in the other and the other in myself. I see the other as a self-determining being who is worthy of respect. A self-determined being thus may well be a moral being on Aboulafia's account. Consideration of Kohlberg's stages of moral development provides support for this conclusion. While Kohlberg did not examine the growth of subjectivity or autonomy in developing his moral stage theory, his stages resemble Aboulafia's in some respects. This resemblance may occur because both theories were inspired by Mead's view of the importance of role taking in the development of the self. For Mead, the self is both a cognitive and a social product, though not an affective one. Interestingly, Kohlberg and Aboulafia both differ with Mead in agreeing that the process of role taking is an affectual development as well. Kohlberg, in fact, maintains that the role taking required for achieving any particular level of moral development cannot occur without the prerequisite level of empathy.

Kohlberg's moral stage theory was also inspired by James Baldwin, John Dewey, and Jean Piaget. While I will not elaborate on their extensive influence on Kohlberg, it is worth noting that Baldwin's theory suggested to Kohlberg the possibility of a psychological explanation of the development of moral ideals. According to Baldwin, the self develops through imitation of others (rather than role playing). This process culminates in the construction of an ideal self, which the person wishes to realize after discovering the inconsistencies of the adult authoritative selves that she previously imitated. The ideal self is an essential component of a person's conscience, and Baldwin believes that it is the main determinant of moral action, rather than rules or consequences.

While Kohlberg favors the idea of role playing to imitation as the basis for the development of the self, Baldwin's story of the construction of the ideal self is found in Kohlberg's three principal moral levels—the preconventional, conventional, and postconventional, which I will explain. It is also worth noting that Baldwin, like Aboulafia and Kohlberg, believes that humans are innately social beings.

It is not my intention to defend the meta-ethical and normative assumptions Kohlberg makes in his psychological research about moral development. However, I think the reader should be aware of these assumptions. His meta-ethical assumptions include the following: (1) moral concepts are not value-neutral; (2) phenomenalism, or the idea that moral judgments are consciously constructed; (3) the universality of moral development; (4) the prescriptivity of "ought" statements; (5) cognitivism, or the idea that moral judgments are not merely expressions of emotion; (6) formalism, or the idea that there are formal qualities of moral judgments that can be agreed on regardless of whether there is agreement on substantive matters; (7) principledness, or the idea that moral judgments rest on the application of general rules and principles; (8) constructivism, or the idea that moral judgments are human constructions generated in social interaction; and (9) the primacy of justice in the moral domain (i.e., that the central concern of morality pertains to the resolution of conflicts). One of his key normative-ethical assumptions is the conception of a moral point of view or an ideal of justice reasoning, which is most adequately expressed at the highest level of development. At the highest level are found attributes of reversibility (i.e., the ability to take the other's perspective), impartiality, universality, and the effort and willingness to come to agreement or consensus with other humans about what is right. Also found is a belief in the Golden Rule (Kohlberg 1983, 8-10).

Kohlberg's ideal of justice reasoning is based on the belief that a higher stage is a better stage than a lower stage in solving problems of conflicting interests and claims, and in particular justice claims. He focuses on justice because, first, situations requiring a choice between conflicting norms or rights elicits generalized reasons or reasoning whose structure can be analyzed and used to define "structural stages" and, second, many western philosophers, such as Plato, Aristotle, Kant, Hume, and Mill, have seen justice as the first or central moral virtue of individuals and societies. Further, western philosophers have regarded justice as rational to the extent that good and compelling reasons can be given for principles of justice. Kohlberg believes that the one underlying principle of justice which underlies all other justice principles is Kantian respect for persons, and it is a principle central to Stage 6 (which was originally his highest stage). The need for rational principles arises from the fact that reasoning about justice is required to resolve the basic conflicts between persons in society. While persons may differ in their views of the good life or of special relations of care and friendship, social life requires some consensus about justice. Kohlberg believes that the ideal toward which justice reasoning moves is that of universal agreement of all persons potentially involved in a justice conflict by means of dialogue and discussion regarding common principles rather than by coercion or manipulation. He refers to Rawls' depiction of persons in the original position interested in a fair choice of principles and Habermas' "ideal communication situation" as examples of situations in which ideal justice reasoning and the moral point of view are fully realized.[3]

Kohlberg's assumptions have been useful in orienting his empirical study of moral development of justice reasoning, but he admits that they remain controversial at a philosophical level. While he admits that they can never be philosophically proven, he provides a strong inductive case for his assumptions in his discussion of alternative accounts of moral development. These other accounts, particularly from the behaviorist or positivist perspective (e.g., Skinnerian) and the "irrationalist" perspective (e.g., Marx, Freud, and Durkheim) make questionable meta-ethical assumptions of their own, which have actually been contradicted by empirical research.

Like his predecessors, Kohlberg's theory can be described in Habermas' terms as a "rational reconstruction of ontogenesis" or an explanation of the movement toward the kind of morality persons striving toward rationality might agree on (Kohlberg 1987, 262). As such, each moral stage is an improvement on the prior one in terms of rationality. Each new stage reflects a higher level of rationality. Kohlberg makes clear, however, that improvements in cognition alone are not sufficient for a person to move to the next stage. Movement between stages requires increasing complexity in role taking, which involves improvements in empathic ability. Expanded opportunities for role playing with parents and peers increase a person's empathic abilities, and Kohlberg discusses studies in which students who had such opportunities were found to be at a more advanced moral stage than students who had not (Kohlberg 1987, 312-313).

Kohlberg assumes with Mead that advances in human development are advances in communications of meanings. Consequently, in his research Kohlberg employs a hermeneutic methodology that adopts an interpretive stance toward the communications of other persons. Thus, he assumes that the child has a rational (or "making sense") attitude in constructing her moral judgments, her rationality is developing, and that her reasons can be understood by persons at higher stages through such means as direct questioning.

Through his research, Kohlberg initially distinguished three principal levels of moral development, with each level consisting of two stages.[4] The second stage at each level is regarded as a more advanced and organized form of the general perspective of that level. It is an advance in cognitive reconstruction and empathizing. To explain the stages, it is helpful to start with an explanation of the levels in which they are found.

The first level is referred to as Preconventional, and research has indicated that it is the level of most children under age nine, some adolescents, and many adolescent and adult criminal offenders. At this level rules and social expectations are external, and it explains the "ought" entirely from a "personal individual" social perspective. The social perspective for each stage is a single unifying construct that generates the major structural features of that stage. In the case of the Preconventional level, the "ought" only refers to an obligation to meet one's own needs. Persons at this level lack the sense of affiliation found at the next level.

The second level is the Conventional, and it is where most adults and adolescents are found. At the Conventional level, persons conform to and uphold the rules and expectations of society simply because they are society's rules and expectations. The social perspective at this level explains the "ought" from the perspective of being a member of society who is concerned about the welfare of his group and who has a sense of affiliation with his group.

The third level is the Postconventional, and it is found in a minority of adults, usually after age twenty. The person at this level understands and accepts society's rules, but the acceptance is derived from accepting the principles that underlie these rules. She resolves conflicts of justice by principle rather than convention and is able to differentiate her values from the rules and expectations of others. She defines her values in terms that may sometimes conflict with those of society. Her "ought" is derived from a "prior-to-society" social perspective. It is "prior-to-society" in the sense that "it is the perspective of an individual who has made the moral commitments or holds the standards on which a good or just society must be based" (Kohlberg 1987, 288). The Postconventional level seems to emerge with the comprehension and acceptance of a contractarian morality.

Since I am chiefly concerned with the moral development of criminal offenders who participate in correctional counseling, I will not more fully explain or defend the existence and order of Kohlberg's higher stages. These have come under some attack in the philosophical literature, but I am not aware of criticisms of his construction of the lower stages. It is sufficient to consider how persons develop at the lower stages to show how increases in cognitive and empathic ability make the typical criminal offender an increasingly moral (and autonomous) individual.

In his chart of the six moral stages, Kohlberg describes the first stage within the Preconventional level as one of "Heteronomous Morality." The person at this stage conceives of "the right thing" as not breaking rules that are backed by punishment and avoiding physical damage to persons and property. He is motivated to do the right thing only out of fear of punishment and the superior power of authorities. His social perspective is egocentric. He has no regard for the interests of others; he does not even recognize that they differ from his own. Actions are considered only in terms of their physical consequences and their bearing on his own interests because there is no comprehension of the interests of others. At this stage there is little empathy, and the authority that provides the reason for doing right is only comprehended, in a sense, as a thing holding a big stick.

Recall my discussion of rationality in chapter 1. Persons whom we may punish must have sufficient rationality for this first stage. Only persons who can at least understand that they will suffer adverse consequences if they commit a particular action are subject to punishment. They must be able to see the threat of punishment as a reason not to commit an offense.

The rationality of the Stage 1 person comprehends a simplistic level of justice reasoning. The person at this stage appreciates distributive justice only as a dictate to divide goods equally. He also understands a justice of reciprocity or of returning bad with punishment and good with reward. In other words, "justice" means only equal distribution of goods, and it is accepted only because it is enforced by punishment. The person at this level sees that it is in his interest to share with others because he will suffer if he refuses to, not because he values justice for its own sake. He also realizes that injustice will be reciprocated with punishment. He does not want to be just, he only wants to avoid punishment, which he can only do by acting justly. He, thus, has two discrete conceptions of justice, a justice of equal distribution and a justice of punishment, which are not fully integrated. It is only at the next stage that they become integrated.

At the second stage within the Preconventional level is the stage of individualism, instrumental purpose, and exchange. It is a stage of advanced prudentiality because the person at this level recognizes that other persons have different interests and that these conflict with his. Right is relative at this stage in a concrete individualistic sense. The right thing for a person to do is to follow rules, but only when it is to his immediate interest, and to act to serve his own interests and needs while letting others do the same. At this stage a bargaining of interests occurs, and right becomes for the person what's fair or an equal exchange between interested parties. The Stage 2 person is motivated to do the right thing in order to serve his own interests because he realizes he lives in a world where others have their own separate interests too. The other is not merely a thing with a stick but a thing that has its own interests, which must be taken into account. Here we begin to see a cognitive and empathic advance in comprehending the other at least as a thing with interests just as one has interests.

The advance to at least the second stage can be referred to as the goal of the moral education of punishment. While persons at the second stage, like the first, see moral requirements as external to themselves, they are better equipped to comprehend the importance of accepting the need to only take moral means to their ends. They are better able to comprehend the requirements of prudence because they have a better understanding of other persons. They have gained this understanding through a primitive form of role taking because to be able to see rightness as an exchange between the competing interests of individual actors requires one to take to some extent the role of the other in order to acquire knowledge of his interests.

Kohlberg says that the person at Stage 2 has a more integrated conception of justice than Stage 1. At Stage 2, a person regards individuals as potentially equal (insofar as they have bargaining power) in having the right to achieve their goals or needs and as having obligations to give these up based on concrete reciprocity. Thus, the justice of dividing goods equally is integrated with the justice of reciprocity. There is an awareness of a rational basis for punishment for a failure of reciprocity.

The person at Stage 3 who has entered the level of conventional morality has made a big leap from the first level. She has begun to internalize moral ends. At Stage 3 the Golden Rule is first accepted, while the Golden Rule for the previous stage means only do to the other what he has done to you. Thus, the second level lacks, in Kohlberg's terms, a more ideal equity. The third stage is hoped for in the moral education of offenders, but it is not required to justify punishment. At Stage 3 the person loses her egocentricity and becomes genuinely interested in the welfare of other persons with whom she is in a relationship. The Golden Rule is still understood very concretely at this stage since it does not extend to abstract others, but in big contrast with the previous stage, relationships with certain others take precedence over selfish interests.

It is not possible, Kohlberg claims, to attain this first stage of the Conventional level without having first progressed through the two stages of the Preconventional level. Before a person can attain the level of role playing, which entails a full empathic identification with another, one must first recognize that there is another who will punish and that that other has interests which conflict with one's own. Hence, we see that advances in prudential rationality are essential to the development of moral judgment, as I claimed in the previous chapter.

It can, of course, be objected that advances in moral judgment may not reflect advances in moral action, and that a person who perceives certain reasons that make actions right may not act on those reasons. Kohlberg makes an interesting reference to a review of the empirical research on the moral stages by A. Blasi (Kohlberg 1987, 306). Blasi found that the higher the stage of moral reasoning, the more likely action will be consistent with the choice made on a moral dilemma. The implication of this finding is that persons at the lowest stage are the least likely to act on the basis of moral judgment. In other words, persons at Stage 1 who find a reason to do the right thing only on the basis of the threat of punishment are most likely to act contrary to it. That is, they will not be strongly deterred by the threat of punishment, which is their only reason for acting morally. Persons at Stage 2 should behave less inconsistently than persons at Stage 1 because they find their moral judgments more compelling. In consequence, persons at Stage 2 should be more morally advanced in terms of their actions as well as their judgments. On the same grounds, we should expect Stage 3 to be a moral advance over Stage 2 in terms of actions as well as judgments.

Blasi's research thus implies that moral education that promotes the cognitive and empathic development of offenders should improve their behavior as well.

PARALLELS BETWEEN ABOULAFIA'S
AND KOHLBERG'S ACCOUNTS

The fact that Aboulafia and Kohlberg were both inspired by Mead in their accounts of the development of the self has already been mentioned. However, the fact that their projects focused on explaining the development of different properties in human beings created an important difference in how their theories took shape. Their projects were also affected by the fact that Mead did not provide an adequate explanation of either human subjectivity or freedom or the moral point of view. Hence, in explaining self-determination, Aboulafia supplemented Mead's account by heeding the arguments of Sartre regarding the development of the not-self, and in explaining the moral point of view, Kohlberg heeded the arguments of Baldwin regarding the development of the ideal self.

It is of interest, however, that both Aboulafia and Kohlberg find significant improvements in the development of the property each is examining when there are increased opportunities for role taking by individuals with persons in authority over them (such as parents) and peers. These increased opportunities seem to improve the development of the object-self greatly, and in turn to improve a person's capacity for envisioning the possibility of new, not yet achieved selves in the future. In the development of the object-self, the individual becomes more adept at internalizing the perspective of the other, and thereby becomes more sympathetic to the other's worth and needs.

In describing the transition between the moral stages, Kohlberg claims that each stage is an improvement in role taking and reversibility over the previous one and that there is no inherent opposition between the stages (i.e., that a later stage of moral judgment does not contradict the previous stage). This claim seems consistent with Mead's views. Mead recognizes no internal conflicts in the growth of the self. In contrast, Aboulafia says that conflict is essential to self-development because it is out of the conflict between impulse and prohibition that choice first develops. It is also the conflict inspired by the existence of negation that first helps differentiate the self from the other. Kohlberg, in not taking into account the presence of conflict in self-development, thus appears to be unable to explain the growth of autonomy in his moral stages. However, I believe that movement along Kohlberg's stages implies not only a more developed object-self but also a more developed not-self. The moral person has also fully internalized negation. Kohlberg's stages can be interpreted as reflecting growth in autonomy as well as growth in moral judgment.

Recall that for Aboulafia, self-determination requires several things: it requires the development of an object-self, the development of a not-self or the internalization of negation through beginning to see the world as a world of possibility, the capacity to reflect on what one is not, and mutual recognition or intersubjectivity.

At Kohlberg's first stage, the individual clearly has a meager object-self. She is unable to differentiate her interests from that of others, and she thereby lacks the perspective of others. She experiences natural impulses which are thwarted by prohibitions backed by punishment. She has sufficient rationality to recognize the consequences of acting on these impulses as a reason not to so act, but the source of these consequences is only understood as a superior power, like a Master in Hegel's terms, which treats her as a mere object. She sees the prohibitions as whips or clubs meant to deter her from acting on impulses that are physically damaging to others. She has some understanding that physical damage to persons and things is bad because she can experience pain and a sense of loss when things she wants are destroyed. However, she does not comprehend psychological damage because as yet she has little sense of self. Her self at this stage consists of a collection of impulses, some of which have been thwarted by a powerful other. She believes that this other dislikes pain and loss like herself, but she does not yet conceive of the punishment she receives at the hands of the other as a consequence of her own behavior. She does not yet see the other as having interests that conflict with her own. In lacking knowledge of the perspective of the other, she consequently has little capacity to predict how the other will behave. In lacking this knowledge, she has little comprehension of her own possibilities. Thus, she also has little freedom. It is no wonder that she is least likely to act on the basis of her moral judgments. She is least likely to own them.

The individual at Stage 1 is particularly vulnerable. The rules she obeys because they are imposed by powerful authority seem completely arbitrary to her. Being viewed as arbitrary, they have no rational basis for her, and they seem capable of changing at any time entirely on the whim of authority. She is in a fearful position. It is only by beginning to comprehend the perspective of authority that she will be able to adequately mollify her fears and predict the basis from which authority will next limit her.

In moving toward Stage 2, Kohlberg says that the individual's cognitive capacities develop to where they are able to integrate two discrete senses of justice into a unified (though not ideal) justice orientation involving concrete mutual reciprocity or an instrumental exchange. At this stage he has some awareness that other people have separate interests and needs which conflict with his own. From this awareness comes a new sense of empowerment. In recognizing that others have their own interests and needs, a person has a better chance of predicting what they will do. He will have a better chance of meeting his own needs. His object-self at this stage is beginning to develop through an awareness of others' interests, though the other remains an object to him in the sense that the other's interests remain external to his self. It can be said that he regards the other like a business associate whom he placates by trying to meet his interests in order to serve his own. He aids the other under the assumption that the other is just as self-serving as he is. He recognizes that this associate will place barriers in his way, but he assumes that these barriers are self-serving. In recognizing that they are self-serving, he has discovered a means of controlling the other. He can work out a deal. He can do this because he has made a cognitive and empathic advance. He has taken on the role of other in the sense that he now recognizes the other's separate interests. However, there is as yet no possibility of mutual recognition because the other remains objectified, and the recognition is one-sided. That is, the other is viewed as completely controlled by his self-serving interests.

A crisis occurs, however, for the person at Stage 2 when he encounters behavior that is not entirely self-serving. When the other places prohibitions or limits that in no way advance her own interests, her behavior can no longer be predicted or controlled. This situation is most notable in the developing child when she becomes aware that her parent places limits on her behavior not for the parent's benefit but out of regard for the child's welfare. The loving parent's behavior seems unpredictable at Stage 2 because it is not self-serving. Rather, the loving parent's prohibitions are solely aimed at promoting the child's welfare and growth. With this experience, the child at Stage 2 encounters a new role—a new way of being, which she can only comprehend if she internalizes and accepts it for herself. It is a way of being-for-others as well as being-for-oneself. She has the choice of refusing to internalize this new role, but if she does, she restricts her own capacity for further self-determination and for determining and shaping the behavior of others. She remains in a sense a slave to a constricted sense of self. However, with acceptance comes a new sense of freedom in the possibility of mutual recognition. Now, the parent's behavior is predictable because the child understands that the parent has conceived of the possibility of what she would want to happen to her if she were the child. The other, the loving parent, has taken on the role of the child. By taking on the role of the parent, the child begins to perceive how the parent's greater knowledge and experience equips the parent to truly benefit the child. The child also begins to comprehend the power of love. Through loving the other herself, through being concerned with the other's benefit, she is now more empowered to predict the other's behavior because it has become her own.

At Stage 3 the person believes in the Golden Rule and is motivated to follow moral dictates because of her concern for others and of her concern to be valued by them. Kohlberg says at this stage that the person believes that "being good" is important and means having good motives and showing concern for others. It also means keeping mutual relationships that are founded on trust, loyalty, respect, and gratitude. This is the first stage in which mutual recognition is a possibility. However, it is not a fully reflective stage in that persons at Stage 3 have not yet generalized the other to consider a societal point of view as well as an interpersonal point of view and in that their conception of good behavior remains stereotypical. Parental and societal prohibitions have yet to be rationally examined. Stage 3 is on the road to Kohlberg's moral ideal, but further advances in reversibility are still possible.

While I believe that further advances along Kohlberg's stages reflect further increases in autonomy, I will not argue that here. For my purposes, it is sufficient to show that improvement in moral judgments between the first three stages also reflect improvement in self-determination. Many criminal offenders are found in the first two stages. Not many are found in the third stage. To make that advance it seems requisite that a person has the experience of being restrained by a caretaker who is truly interested in promoting her autonomy. Aboulafia says that parents can defeat the child's potential autonomy by refusing to recognize his "no" and by not giving the child a world to affect and shape. He says that parents do so by being overly indulgent as well as being overly restrictive because the child's "no" has as little meaning when it is always heeded as when it is always ignored (Aboulafia, 113). In always heeding the child's "no," I think the parent also errs in not allowing her the opportunity to begin to comprehend that parental prohibition has a rational basis. Its rational basis is first discovered at Stage 2 when it is seen as a means of protecting the parent's interests, but it is better understood at Stage 3 when it is seen as the parent's means of benefiting the child.

Since many criminal offenders come from families with overly restrictive or overly indulgent parents, it is not surprising that they should have much difficulty getting past the Preconventional level. With a history of parental indifference to the needful setting of appropriate limits, they have little reason to believe that the state, which is a more impersonal authority, should care about benefiting them. On the other hand, as I have argued, they should have the opportunity through state punishment of making a moral advance by learning why they must behave more prudentially, and the moral education of punishment can at least aim at promoting the instrumental rationality of Stage 2.

Each of Kohlberg's stages reflects different degrees of self-determination because each stage reflects a different degree of self-definition and empowerment. At the first stage we find a person with little self-definition because she cannot adequately differentiate her interests from that of others. Definition requires a boundary or limit, and she knows no distinctions to establish that limit. She does know that pain and loss are bad and best avoided. She also knows that violations of prohibitions established by a powerful other result in bad consequences to her. Thus, she finds in anticipation of these consequences a reason to behave. However, unlike an animal, she is not conditioned to behave in certain ways. She does not merely slink back at prohibition. She can choose to risk the consequences of the punishment that may befall her. In fact, according to Blasi's research, this choice may even happen frequently among persons at her level. Thus, she is free due to this choice but in a very constricted sense. She has the minimal freedom of the pre-reflective consciousness.

At the next stage the other is perceived as more differentiated in having separate interests, yet also more similar in having the desire to have his interests met. The other is like a business associate whom one is able to negotiate with in terms of balancing interests. In that the other is more differentiated, there is a clearer boundary for the self and a clearer understanding of what the self may be able to achieve.

Further differentiation of the other occurs when the person realizes that not all of the other's behavior is self-serving but results from a concern for her welfare. With recognition of this new role, she realizes a new way of being and of interacting with others. In accepting the Golden Rule, revolutionary growth occurs in her self because the rules she has merely obeyed in the past out of fear or self-interest have now become her own. Through increasing empathic identification with the other and cognitive reconstruction of roles, she has begun to freely define herself as a person with a moral point of view.

THE SOLUTION TO THE
PUZZLE AND ANOTHER PROBLEM

In considering the levels of autonomy found in Kohlberg's stages, we can now answer the puzzle about how a person can be both free and unfree. A criminal offender who is at Stage 1 is free in the sense that he can consider the threat of punishment a reason not to commit an offense. He is free in that he can consider alternative means of accomplishing his ends, which will not result in punishment, and in that he can also choose to risk the punishment. However, he is also unfree because he lacks knowledge of the perspective of those in power over him, and their actions ultimately seem arbitrary to him. It is only when he recognizes the rational basis for their interest in his following the rules that he is no longer a slave to their rules. This is a recognition that can only occur with the empathic and cognitive advance that leads to Stage 2. At Stage 2, he has acquired the power of the negotiator.

In chapter 2 I promised a more complete answer to the last horn of Shafer-Landau's dilemma in this chapter. Shafer-Landau poses the problem that if we claim that moral autonomy is an inalienable right, then we are not free to give up our moral freedom. In the present chapter I have shown how freedom develops in persons through social interaction by means of the development of the object-self and the not-self and that as freedom develops persons become increasingly capable of (and interested in) choosing the good. Moral autonomy is an inalienable right because it reflects empathic and cognitive capacities that cannot be reversed short of brain surgery. While persons at the higher stages of moral autonomy can comprehend the rational perspective of the lower stages, they recognize that the lower stages arise from a much more limited perspective of the other. They cannot reverse their progress without becoming much less than they are. A reversal would make them less rational and less emotionally connected to others. Further, a human without some degree of moral autonomy or the hope of achieving it is clearly an unenviable object. Such a being would probably be the product of extreme social isolation and/or profound mental retardation.

In concluding this chapter, I would like to stress that there is one philosopher whose philosophical insights made possible the insights of Merleau-Ponty, Mead, Sartre, Aboulafia, Baldwin, and Kohlberg in explaining the development of the self. Each of these philosophers were greatly influenced by Hegel's philosophy of stages. Without Hegel's analysis of the development of self-consciousness within a social and historical milieu, none of these insights would have been possible. Hegel, of course, owes something to Aristotle and Kant. Another philosopher deserves some credit too. Mead and Baldwin both derived their notions of the self as an evolving organism from Darwin.

In the next chapter I will argue that persons engaged in correctional counseling do aim at the goal of self-determination in the inmates they counsel by reviewing some of the current literature in the field of correctional counseling. I will show that an advance in prudentiality and autonomy as evidenced by the acquisition of the cognitive and empathetic abilities required for at least Stage 2 moral judgment is an important aim of this type of counseling.

NOTES

1. For the most part, in this section I synthesize ideas expressed by Mitchell Aboulafia in Part II of *The Mediating Self*, pages 73–126.

2. In this section much of the description of Kohlberg's moral stage theory and the philosophical theories which inspired it is drawn from chapters 6 and 7 of his *Child Psychology and Childhood Education* (1987), p. 223–328.

3. See Kohlberg, *Child Psychology and Childhood Education*, 1987, p. 292–294.

4. Later research revealed a seventh stage. He also later theorized that there are two substages within each stage, a heteronomous and an autonomous substage.

Chapter Five

Self-Determination as a Goal of Correctional Counseling

This chapter concludes my principal defense of the claim that self-determination is a goal of correctional counseling. This has been shown to be a possible goal because punishment is partly justified as a means of morally educating offenders, because punishment can improve offenders' lives by improving their capacity for self-determination, and because self-determination admits of degrees. A person becomes increasingly self-determined as her cognitive and empathic capacities for perceiving herself from the role of the other and for perceiving herself as a person capable of changing into a new way of being improves.

My present task is to show that persons who are actually practicing correctional counseling are concerned with facilitating such improvements in self-determination in their offender clients. To do so, I commence by examining the activity of correctional counseling as it has been discussed in some of the recent literature in the field in order to arrive at a fairly precise definition. It includes the requirement that persons doing correctional counseling have a specific theoretical orientation regarding the psychological cause and treatment of criminal behavior.

There are several predominating psychological theories that have guided the development of treatment techniques with offenders. These theories differ in their explanation of the cause of criminal behavior with varying emphases placed on early childhood experience, emotion, thought, and behavior. These differing explanations of the source of the problem have led the theories' proponents in different treatment directions. While the differences are notable, I intend to show that correctional counselors from all of these theoretical orientations intend that their clients become more fully self-determining.

I am grouping the psychological theories into four general areas: psychoanalytic, phenomenological-existentialist, behaviorist, and rational. It is my contention that any person involved in correctional counseling operates from one (or more, if she is an eclectic) of these theoretical orientations. There are numerous therapies that could be said to fall under these general categories. However, only certain therapies from these four have been discussed in the literature as having been used with offender-clients. Consequently, I am limiting my discussion within each general theoretical orientation to more specific theories that have dictated actual treatment modalities with offenders.

It is not my purpose here to rate the moral correctness or relative effectiveness of any of the treatment modalities mentioned. Each has had its detractors. In terms of effectiveness, Louis Carney says that psychotherapy is "an art, or an art combined with a science, which may transcend the empirical boundaries that confine science" (111). In other words, scientific research has a limited ability to measure therapeutic success. This has been particularly evident when correctional treatment success has been monitored in the usual manner by studying recidivism rates. Such studies have been fraught with much controversy in recent decades, and it certainly seems doubtful that such an external measure (even when accurately determined) could fully measure the internal change reflected by improvements in self-determination.

DEFINING CORRECTIONAL COUNSELING

In order to examine the activity of correctional counseling, I first consider the larger project that correctional counseling is intended to be a part of—corrections. This is important because correctional counseling can be defined most broadly as the counseling of persons who are criminal offenders within state correctional settings. The term "corrections" seems to refer to all modern forms of state punishment (except perhaps capital punishment), and it connotes the idea of correcting what has been mistaken, whether in attitude or behavior. I defined punishment in the first chapter as a response to the wrongdoing of a rational person which not only interferes with her freedom to fulfill her desires but which is also intended to induce suffering (in order to motivate change). In his book, *Correctional Counseling and Treatment*, Peter Kratcoski offers a somewhat similar definition for corrections. He says that corrections means "to change a condition that is considered to be undesirable or has been a mistake and to bring things back to a state that is considered desirable or appropriate" and that it involves the care, custody, and supervision of convicted offenders (3). Contrary to my view, however, his definition reflects the belief that the primary goal of state corrections is only to make offenders law-abiding or to behave in the manner conventional authority finds desirable or appropriate. The goal of benefiting the offender is secondary and a mere means to the primary goal. This view leaves Kratcoski with no nonarbitrary reason for limiting the scope of correctional treatment to humane forms. For instance, he has no legitimate reason for excluding drastic forms of psychosurgery from corrections, such as that which would turn a person into a lap dog. As I argue in previous chapters, justified punishment cannot be limited to meeting the goal of self-protection. I will speak at greater length about the nonrelativistic goals of counseling in the next chapter.

While David Lester and Michael Braswell bow to convention in entitling their book *Correctional Counseling*, they prefer the term "offender counseling" to describe the activity of counselors in correctional settings. They fear that the term "correctional counseling" does not reflect an interest by the counselor in helping offenders with the outside world as much as in helping them adjust to prison life. In the case of parole and probation officers, they fear that the term may emphasize their enforcement or case management role rather than their responsibility to *therapeutically* correct offenders. They seem to eschew the notion of corrections in the counseling of offenders, which Kratcoski endorses as an interest in changing the offender to meet the needs of authority. Rather, their term "offender counseling" connotes a therapeutic intervention with offender clients. Being therapeutic, the intervention is intended to be of real benefit to the client (Lester and Braswell, 3).

Lester and Braswell also express the concern that "correctional counseling" is misleading in that in many cases one may wonder whether counselors can "correct" offenders if they want to. Hence, they prefer to say that these counselors are "helping professionals who attempt to apply their skills and expertise in correctional and related settings" (3). Note that this description fits my justification of punishment in which I indicate that punishers must intend (or attempt) to morally educate those they punish. Clearly, Lester and Braswell agree that offender (or correctional) counselors are truly interested in benefiting their offender clients. In fact, they are correct, because, while there is no guarantee in any case that this goal will be met, such counseling always aims at improving the life of the client, at helping.

With this view of counseling, Lester and Braswell's concerns about the term "correctional counseling" can be answered. If we assume that within the field of corrections, there are helping professionals who mean to positively intervene in the lives of offenders, then the correcting activity they perform is meant to directly benefit the offenders and not simply the detaining authority. Hence, while "correctional counseling" appears to have some troublesome connotations, the term need not be abandoned.

Correctional counseling also falls under the general category of correctional treatment. Kratcoski defines correctional treatment as "any planned and monitored program of activity that has the goal of rehabilitating or 'habilitating' the offender so that he or she will avoid criminal activity in the future" (4). He is correct that correctional treatment—or what has been commonly referred to as rehabilitation programs within corrections—consists of a wide variety of planned activities. These can include alcohol and drug treatment, AA and NA meetings, GED classes, college classes, recreational programs, and vocational training, as well as a wide array of psychological services, which can be described as forms of correctional counseling. However, he is incorrect in implying that the only goal of these programs is to make the offender avoid criminal behavior in the future. John Stratton says that if you ask any correctional worker why he decided on his profession, one of the most common responses will be that "I wanted to help people" (24). Carney confirms this view by stating that the ultimate goal of treatment expressed by correctional staff is "restoration" because "corrections is designed to impel man toward his fullness and not his emptiness" (41).

Correctional counseling also falls under the general category of counseling or psychotherapy. The distinction between counseling and psychotherapy is not important here. Counseling psychologists usually refer to their interactions with clients as counseling, while clinical psychologists refer to theirs as psychotherapy. The distinction between the two professions has traditionally had only to do with their client populations. Counseling psychologists work with "normal" clients and clinical psychologists with "abnormal" clients or those who are diagnosable according to the *Diagnostic and Statistical Manual* of the American Psychiatric Association. However, there is much overlap in these professions. Hence, I am treating the terms synonymously because both counselors and psychotherapists work within the same group of theoretical orientations, and they use many of the same treatment approaches.

Cecil Patterson also finds little substantial difference between counseling and psychotherapy in his *Theories of Counseling and Psychotherapy*. He says that both are "processes involving a special kind of relationship between a person who asks for help with a psychological problem (the client or the patient) and a person who is trained to provide that help (the counselor or the therapist)" (xii). Objectives of counseling and psychotherapy may vary due to the nature of the problem addressed and the theoretical orientation of the counselor or therapist. However, there is a common goal that Patterson says that counselors and therapists hold which The Committee on Definition, Division of Counseling Psychology of the American Psychological Association describes. It says that counselors intend to "help individuals toward overcoming obstacles to their personal growth, wherever these may be encountered, and toward achieving optimum development of their personal resources" (Patterson, xiii). From Patterson, it thus appears that counseling entails a relationship between two persons in which one of the persons (the client) has a psychological problem impeding her growth which she has some interest in changing, and the other person (the helping professional) is interested in aiding the client in overcoming this problem.

In the process of assisting the client, however, Carney clarifies that the counselor is not a change *agent* because change cannot take place without initiation by the client. Rather, he says that counselors are really change facilitators. As change facilitators, he goes on to say, counselors must have the healing power to empower and offset the powerlessness of the client. He describes power here as the capacity to control one's destiny. So, in his view, counseling in general is interested in making clients self-determining. I agree with Carney even though he does not prove these claims, and they may be regarded as questionable from certain therapeutic orientations that do not appear to endorse the notion of human freedom. As I will eventually show, self-determination is an important goal from any of these (Carney, 149).

It can be objected at this point that the discussion of counseling as a relationship in which one party desires assistance with addressing a specific problem may rule out many forms of correctional counseling where clients are coerced into attending counseling. This objection, however, is mistaken. When a person is coerced into counseling, it does not necessarily follow that she has no motivation and will not acquire any motivation to change, and it consequently does not follow that she cannot benefit from the counseling. Further, many nonoffender clients are coerced into counseling by employers, family, or friends, and in many of these cases, the clients come to understand the need for counseling and to benefit from it. The presence of coercion does not, therefore, preclude the possibility that counseling is taking place. Only if the purported client is coerced into conversing with a counselor, she has no motivation to change, and she has no capacity to acquire this motivation can it be said that only the appearance of counseling, but not real counseling, is occurring.

From the preceding, we may say that correctional counseling is a process involving a relationship between two persons. One of those persons is a criminal offender who has been placed in a state correctional setting and who has a psychological problem that impedes her growth and that she has (or will have) some interest in changing even if she has been in some way coerced into the relationship. The other person is a helping professional who is interested in facilitating the client's desired change. Lester and Braswell provide a similar definition. They define correctional (offender) counseling as

an intensive, purposeful interactive process between a counselor who is professionally prepared to deal with the special problems posed by a correctional environment and a client who has been found guilty of committing a crime or act of delinquency and placed in a correctional institution, facility, or agency (182).

The Lester and Braswell definition adds the requirement that the person doing the counseling have some special knowledge of appropriate psychological interventions and the specific needs of an offender clientele. It also more clearly extends the purview of correctional counseling to include counseling by probation or parole officers and other counselors working with offender clients in community agencies. These further clarifications regarding the activity of correctional counseling are important because it is neither necessary nor sufficient to have the title of "correctional counselor" to be a person involved in correctional counseling.

According to the *Manual of Correctional Standards* (1975) by the American Correctional Association (ACA), correctional counseling is

> a relationship in which one endeavors to help another and solve his problems of adjustment. It is distinguished from advice or admonition in that it implies *mutual* consent. As the term has come to be used in working with offenders, counseling encompasses the personal and group relationships undertaken by staff. It has as its goals either the immediate solution of a specific personal problem or a long-range effort to develop increased self-understanding and maturity within the offender. Counseling may be part of the activity of professional casework or psychiatric staff, but is also the proper province of the teacher, the work supervisor, and the group supervisor (Carney, 145-146).

Clearly, the ACA does not regard it necessary to have the title of "correctional counselor" in order to be a helping professional involved in correctional counseling. This is consistent with my definition. On the other hand, the ACA does not spell out the knowledge and abilities that are necessary for doing correctional counseling.

Lester and Braswell say that persons doing correctional counseling have certain essential abilities. These seem to be essential if the counseling is going to be effective. They are a sense of timing, effective risking, and a sense of professional humility. Timing within the interactive process of counseling reflects having good communicative abilities; effective risking pertains to aiding the client in a careful cost analysis of alternative behaviors; and professional humility reflects the knowledge that counselors can no more "correct" their clients than that they can guarantee that offenders will be rewarded for making positive socially acceptable decisions. In a way reminiscent of Merleau-Ponty, Lester and Braswell say that counselors should be aware that persons are not free to choose what life brings, but persons are free regarding how they choose to respond to whatever it brings. It is the job of persons doing correctional counseling to be aware of this fact of life and to communicate its truth to their client. This is a means of promoting the client's self-respect (Lester and Braswell, 3-6).

While a course of formal training is not requisite to have these abilities, some form of training may well be necessary for persons doing correctional counseling to understand the offender-client's needs and potential for psychological growth. Carney, for one, says that it is important for persons who work in correctional rehabilitation to have a working knowledge of the major psychotherapies because: (1) correctional treatment involves the practical application of the fruits of behavioral research; (2) such knowledge will assist "correctionalists" in obtaining a clearer perspective on the source of offender's difficulties; (3) the techniques and skills derived from these theories can be learned for use in the treatment setting; and (4) a grounding in these therapies will prepare the person to effectively assist offender-clients in managing life crises and will prevent the client and the practitioner from living what Socrates calls "the unexamined life" (111).

I will go further than Carney because I believe that some working knowledge of the ideas behind the major psychotherapies is not only important to correctional counseling, but it is essential if correctional counseling is going to occur. That is, if the person doing counseling aims to aid the client in overcoming a particular problem, then she must have some idea as to the source of the problem and an appropriate means for addressing it. She must believe that the problem is caused either by reinforcement, early childhood experience, irrational or maladaptive beliefs, or emotional dysfunction. She must think that there is a psychological cause for the problem that can best be identified by either a behaviorist, psychoanalytic, rational, or existentialist-phenomenological approach. These four theoretical orientations comprise the current understanding of possible psychological reasons for maladaptive behavior.

Of course, there are other nonpsychological explanations or models of human behavior, in particular offender behavior, which include the physiological and sociological. The physiological or medical model attributes criminality, for instance, to biochemical, hormonal, or other factors within the central nervous system. The sociological model focuses on society and family dynamics as the cause. The approach to the treatment of criminality within these two models does not principally involve counseling of the individual offender. Rather, the physiological model recommends medical intervention, while the sociological model recommends societal change. The sociological model may also lend itself to family counseling, but such counseling is usually oriented around a particular psycho-theoretical perspective.

Therefore, the ACA is correct in saying that correctional counseling is also the proper province of the correctional teacher, work supervisor, and group supervisor. Insofar as these individuals have some understanding of the psychological source of maladaptive behavior and therapeutic approaches to these problems, then they may be capable of a counseling relationship with certain offenders. For instance, if they are aware that positive work behaviors are promoted through the use of a positive reinforcer such as complimenting the offender for work well done, then they probably have some insight as to at least one theoretical perspective of maladaptive behavior and its treatment.

Besides not being necessary, having the title "correctional counselor" is not sufficient for being a person who does correctional counseling. While correctional institutions in the last twenty years have typically required at least a bachelor's degree in criminal justice, counseling, social work, or some area of the behavioral sciences for persons holding this position, a degree in any area was acceptable in the past. Lester and Braswell report that correctional counselors in prisons in previous decades had a wide variety of majors—from art to accounting to dentistry. Many of these counselors remain employed. It is uncertain whether they have either the knowledge or the interest in performing correctional counseling defined herein. Further, correctional counselors have many diverse job responsibilities within institutional settings besides direct counseling. Some institutions, in fact, clearly deemphasize counseling and other rehabilitative measures because they are chiefly or solely security-oriented. These institutions provide counselors little time, incentive, or support for attempting to counsel offender-inmates (Lester and Braswell, 181-195).

Thus, having the title of "correctional counselor" is neither necessary nor sufficient for a person engaged in correctional counseling. Correctional counseling involves a relationship between two persons, one a convicted offender who needs and desires (or can desire) assistance with a specific problem, and the other a helping professional who wishes to facilitate change in the offender. The helping professional has some knowledge of at least one specific psychological theory of maladaptive behavior and at least one associated treatment modality that he exercises through the counseling process.

CORRECTIONAL PSYCHOLOGICAL THEORIES AND TECHNIQUES

I have contended that correctional counseling is always directed by a specific psychological theoretical orientation and that each has as an objective the self-determination of the client. In the following I review the four major classifications of counseling theory. Each has directed correctional counselors involved in both individual and group counseling with offenders. While my definition of correctional counseling emphasizes counseling as an interaction within an individual relationship between a counselor and a single client, this activity also occurs within group counseling. Group counseling specifically involves therapeutic interactions between a counselor and individuals within a group setting. In the group milieu, the goal of benefiting the individual offender remains of utmost importance, although the direct interaction between counselor and client may be somewhat diffused.

The discussion of each classification is not an exhaustive explanation of the psychological theory and its forms of treatment. Rather, for the purposes of this chapter I focus in each section on the theory's explanation of the source of specifically criminal behavior and the form and goals of treatment for this type of behavior with offender clients. Only theories that have inspired counseling techniques with offenders are described. The descriptions of the theories and techniques are derived chiefly from those of Carney, Lester and Braswell, and Patterson. The descriptions of social learning theory and the very recent cognitivist approaches are derived from that of Van Voorhis, Braswell, and Lester.

PSYCHOANALYSIS AND TRANSACTIONAL ANALYSIS

Freudian Psychoanalysis

While there are many branches of psychoanalytic thought, all have their origins in the theory of Sigmund Freud. Psychoanalytic theories, starting with Freud, explain human behavior on the basis of early childhood experience. They commonly hold that all human behavior is motivated by instinctual desires or desires learned through early experience, generally within the first six years of life. Maladaptive behavior in later life is due to early traumas, losses, frustrations, and deprivations. There are, of course, some nonpsychoanalytic theories that share this view, but these other developmental theories fit into the person-centered or cognitive categories, which I will separately describe. In this section I will focus on the psychoanalytic viewpoint or the therapeutic orientation that grew out of Freudian theory.

Freud was a strict determinist, and consequently it may seem difficult to explain how his theory could account for self-determination. However, I will show that Freudian theory recommends a therapeutic technique that has the end of advancing the sort of self-determining progress I describe in the previous chapter.

Freudian theory, and to a greater or lesser extent, psychoanalytic theories that follow Freud propose that there are three types of desires that motivate all human behavior. First, there are id desires or instinctual desires for self-gratification. Second, there are superego desires, which are those desires that a child acquires through internalizing parental prohibitions on the expression of id desires. In the process of acquiring the superego desires, many id desires become unconscious. Even the most deviant criminal acquires some superego desires insofar as he dresses and eats appropriately. Third, there are ego desires, which are desires acquired through a person's contact with the world. The ego desires function as compromises between id desires, superego desires, and the constraints of the external world. The development of ego desires reflects greater maturity and rationality.

Freudians typically explain criminal behavior as the result of id desires seeking direct gratification in a person who has a poorly developed set of superego desires and weak ego desires. The criminal has
not adequately internalized parental prohibitions on his id desires, and
he has not developed a good set of mature and rational desires that
will enable him to get what he wants. In some cases the criminal behavior may also be a form of displacement as, for example, a Freudian
may say that Oswald really wanted to kill his mother rather than John
F. Kennedy, the head of the "mother" country. Some criminals may
offend in order to get caught like children who misbehave in order to
force the parents to show enough concern to discipline.

Lester and Braswell describe two psychoanalytic techniques that
have been used with the criminal offender. For the intelligent neurotic
offender whose acting out results from improper displacement of
anger toward significant others in his early life, the focus of therapy
is to bring the unconscious id desires into conscious awareness. By
bringing these desires into consciousness, the theory assumes that the
person can begin to learn to live with them through finding socially
acceptable channels for their expression or by simply learning to
avoid those situations in which they could cause problems. Therapy
in this sort of case enhances the development and strength of new ego
desires.

In the case of the delinquent offender whose acting out relates to
poorly developed superego desires or weak ego desires, the focus of
therapy is to promote positive transference between the delinquent
and the therapist. Through learning to identify with a concerned authority figure, the delinquent is given the opportunity to develop appropriate superego controls of his impulses. At the same time, therapy
allows the delinquent the opportunity (perhaps through structured
recreation) for appropriate expression of impulse gratification. In this
way, ego desires are developed to mediate between the needs of the id
desires for expression and the limits of the external world. The delinquent learns rational means for gratifying his id desires.

In the case of the delinquent, it is clear that the psychoanalytic
counselor aims to help the client make advances in self-control by internalizing appropriate superego controls. The client accomplishes
this by internalizing the prohibitions or moral ideals of the therapist.
By doing so, she makes advances toward the conventional morality

of Stage 3 described by Kohlberg. The counselor recognizes that only if the client can be induced in some way to adopt the counselor's perspective can she gain superego controls. As Stage 3 is a more self-determined stage than the lower levels at which we find the offender, who sees moral values as external to herself, the psychoanalytic counselor is clearly interested in making the client more self-determining.

In the case of the intelligent adult neurotic offender, the psychoanalytic counselor is principally interested in strengthening ego desires in order to enhance the client's self-control and reduce the possibility of future offenses. The counselor intends to bring the unconscious irrational desires of the client into consciousness to facilitate the development of rational ego desires. In lacking awareness of the irrational desires, the client lacks the ability to control their expression. The counselor wants to facilitate the growth of rationality by bringing into conscious awareness these desires. This interest in rational self-control also indicates an interest in movement along Kohlberg's hierarchy of levels of moral judgment. In becoming increasingly rational, the client is better able to predict and understand the reactions of others to his behavior in any circumstance and is consequently more self-determined. He is also more in touch with the demands and constraints of conventional morality as he gains greater understanding of his own impulses.

While Freud believes that moral values are only a matter of convention, he does find it rational to accept the dictates of conventional morality. Internalizing these conventions and developing ego desires that sublimate id desires enable a person to get what she wants. Hence, psychoanalytic therapy for criminal offenders is interested in helping these clients advance toward the third stage of Kohlberg's hierarchy of moral judgment. Insofar as the acceptance of conventional morality is rationally dictated, it seems that there is some objective basis for accepting them. The objective basis is that they will enhance one's capacity for self-governance and self-determination.

Transactional Analysis

Transactional analysis (TA) is a psychological theory and therapeutic technique that was developed by Eric Berne, a psychoanalyst, in response to the perceived limitations of traditional psychoanalysis. It shares some features with traditional psychoanalysis in that its description of ego states is highly reminiscent of id, ego, and superego desires. However, TA tends to be more present-oriented and focused on short-term therapeutic change, and it is typically used in group rather than individual counseling. Correctional workers have found TA to be highly practical in correctional settings. Consequently, it has been widely used. As a popular offshoot of psychoanalytic theory, it deserves a section of its own.

TA classifies all human behavior as products of three ego states. Ego states are coherent systems of feelings related to a given object. They can be regarded as coherent sets of behavior patterns or as the feelings that motivate a set of behavior patterns. The Child ego state is the one experienced as a child. It is retained in memory either consciously or unconsciously, and it has childlike properties, such as prelogical thinking and distorted perception. The Parent ego state is the one in which a person's behavior is identifiable with that of his parents. It is judgmental in an imitative way in that it seeks to enforce borrowed values and standards. It is the internalized voice of the parent. The Adult ego state reflects mature, reality-oriented behavior. It is an ego state experienced by adults who are concerned with accurately processing data they encounter as they live. At any point in time TA asserts that one of these ego states is in power and is governing behavior.

I will not address the full complexities of the TA technique, but will instead focus on the goals of TA. Its principal goal is social control. In social control the Adult retains the executive power and is not contaminated by other ego states. Other goals include awareness of things as they really are rather than as you were taught that they are; spontaneity or the freedom to choose and express your feelings rather than playing games; and the ability to have spontaneous game-free awareness of other people. TA is interested in ending self-defeating games. Games are complementary transactions between two people that take place at conscious and unconscious or apparent and ulterior levels. TA aims to teach clients to recognize games and end them and then to help the clients to switch to genuine (i.e., nonmanipulative) and intimate interactions with others.

TA has been quite useful in explaining the manipulative games that prisoners play. In fact, Berne refers to the major game that criminals play as "Cops and Robbers." It originates, like some other psychological disorders, in structural pathology. When there is a structural problem among ego states, one ego state contaminates another. In this particular game, the Child contaminates the Adult so that childlike behavior intrudes into adult-like behavior, but without the person's awareness. The apparent aim of the person playing this game is to get away with the crime, but his ulterior motive is to get caught. The Adult wants the payoff from offending, but it has to lose to the Child who is playing the game of outwitting the cops, so the Child can win. Berne excludes the professional criminal from this explanation, who seems to have no ulterior motives.

In persons with adaptive behavior, the Adult maintains control and chooses appropriate situations in which to act on the impulses of the Child ego state. For criminals, TA holds that typically the Child ego state contaminates the Adult ego state so the person does not see the Child-driven impulses as inappropriate or unjustified in certain situations. It is easy to conceptualize many offenders as persons in whom the Child is in charge, especially when they express no guilt, but for some offenders, the Child and Parent may alternate so that they only feel guilty when the Parent is in charge.

Since TA aims at social control, which involves strengthening the Adult ego state, it aims at reducing the potential for acting out which occurs when the Child is in charge. Hence, TA is interested in promoting responsible behavior. It is also interested in helping the Adult carefully examine the Parent ego state to see whether the Parent is realistic and rational and does not undermine the capacity of the Adult to control the Child.

In its interest in promoting rational and responsible behavior through close analysis of behavior patterns and communications between persons, TA, like traditional psychoanalysis, is interested in the self-determination of clients. It is not interested in how these ego states originally came into being but only with understanding present transactional styles and with eradicating maladaptive ones. In promoting self and other awareness, TA is concerned with improving the client's prudential rationality. In striving to end game-playing, TA is also interested in promoting respect for the values and needs of others. TA wants clients to achieve genuine and intimate relationships with others, which should only be possible if they have to some extent internalized moral values. Hence, TA wants clients to make moral improvements as well.

PHENOMENOLOGICAL–EXISTENTIALIST THERAPY: THE PERSON-CENTERED APPROACH

Existentialism and phenomenology were greatly influential in inspiring the development of a number of twentieth-century theories of psychological counseling, most notably that of Carl Rogers, Rollo May, Fritz Perls, George Kelly, Roy Grinker, and Viktor Frankl. However, in the correctional setting, it is only the theory and technique of Rogers that has been used to any extent. Hence, in this section I will only discuss Roger's person-centered theory and his goals of counseling.

Rogers follows the phenomenological tradition of focusing on the phenomenal world or subjective experience of the client, particularly her self-concept as it has been shaped by her experiences of the world. According to Patterson, however, Rogers differs from the standard phenomenological view in rejecting the implications of strict determinism or the idea that behavior is entirely determined by one's subjective experience of the world. If persons are entirely determined in this manner, it would appear that they could not be free. Instead, Rogers claims that the maladjusted person lacks congruence between his perceived self and his phenomenal world. This person denies significant experience or distorts it in awareness as a defensive reaction to the frustration of his most basic impulses, which are to love, to belong, and to feel secure. In Rogers' view, this person lacks freedom, and it is the point of therapy to increase his freedom. Patterson observes that this conception of freedom within a phenomenological deterministic framework (i.e., being determined by phenomenal experience) is rather problematic. He quotes from Rogers who says:

> We could say that in the optimum of therapy, the person rightfully experiences the most complete and absolute freedom. He wills or chooses to follow the course of action which is the most economical vector in relationship to all the internal and external stimuli, because it is that behavior which will be most deeply satisfying. But this is the

same course of action which from another vantage point may be said to be determined by all the factors in the existential situation. Let us contrast this with the picture of a person who is defensively organized. He wills or chooses to follow a given course of action, but finds that he cannot behave in the fashion he chooses. He is determined by the factors in the existential situation, but these factors include his defensiveness, his denial or distortion of some of the relevant data. Hence it is certain that his behavior will be less than fully satisfying. His behavior is determined, but he is not free to make an effective choice. The fully functioning person, on the other hand, not only experiences, but utilizes, the most absolute freedom when he spontaneously, freely, and voluntarily chooses and wills that which is absolutely determined (Patterson, 408-409).

Patterson rightly criticizes Rogers' claim that the basis for the distinction in being determined is a bit forced, if not moralistic. I will not try to defend Rogers' inconsistency here because I think that freedom as he understands it evolves dynamically from an interaction between a person and the actual world. It is not determined simply by the perceived world. This is because the well-adjusted and free person is rational and realistic. His perceptions must fit with the way the world really is. Consequently, Rogers' inconsistency is not an overwhelming problem for my claim that he is truly interested in promoting self-determination (Patterson, 406-410).

Underlying Rogers' distinction are certain assumptions about human nature and what humans require. Rogers views humans as evolving organisms that have the potential for growth and self-actualization. Self-actualization involves developing all of the capacities that serve to maintain or enhance the organism. In order to self-actualize a person needs to feel positive self-regard and positive regard from others. She satisfies her need for positive regard from others when she perceives herself as satisfying another's need. In encountering other persons she finds, however, that on many occasions, there are conditions placed on whether others find her to be of worth. This merely conditional acceptance can lead to feelings of frustration and incongruence between the perceived self and actual experience (i.e., actual experience may suggest one is less worthy), which in turn can lead to highly defensive behavior that is no longer self-actualizing but is instead self-defeating. It is self-defeating because it is a consequence of distorted perceptions of experience. The person thus develops a distorted view of her own worth and capabilities.

Freedom for Rogers, therefore, seems to pertain chiefly to whether the person's choices promote self-actualization or defeat it. A person is optimally free in his view if he is not defensive because other persons have regarded him as having only conditional value. A person is optimally free if he regards himself as having unconditional positive worth and as being valued unconditionally by others. This unconditional valuing permits him free rein of the capacities he has and the confidence to explore new experiences or new ways of being.

Rogers' conception of freedom can be regarded developmentally and as compatible with the conception of self-determination that I present. For Rogers, the young child grows from having an awareness of her own needs and a coherent interest in satisfying those needs to beginning to differentiate her self from others through experiencing interactions with others in her environment. From this experience of interaction, her self-concept develops, and a need for positive regard from others also develops in order for her to view her self positively. To become fully self-determined she must experience mutual respect. In this development, we can trace some of Aboulafia's stages. The child begins to develop a sense of self through comprehending how others perceive her. Their perceptions, however, will not promote her developing self-determination unless she believes that they perceive her as worthy of respect or as a person who is not a mere object but who is capable of changing and growing.

It is not clear that Rogers believes that the conflicts Aboulafia describes during this developmental process are inevitable. However, it is clear that the thrust of person-centered counseling is to resolve the inner conflicts that are found in maladjusted individuals through providing an environment of mutual respect in the counseling relationship. The key ingredients for person-centered counseling are empathy, unconditional positive regard, and genuineness. The counselor must be a role model who comes to comprehend the client's subjective experiences while at the same time valuing her unconditionally. By this means, the client is freed from her defensiveness and is free to develop a more congruent and organized conception of her self and her experience. Clearly, self-determination in its fullest sense is the optimal goal of person-centered counseling.

In the correctional setting, Lester and Braswell state that person-centered counseling is less popular now than formerly because it does not allow counselors to advise, challenge, confront, or role play. When counseling a highly manipulative offender, person-centered counseling seems much less effective than, for instance, the approach of TA or reality therapy. However, they say that the technique is apparently helpful in crisis counseling, career counseling, counseling with hospitalized alcoholics, improving institutional adjustment, and improving attitudes toward authority figures among parolees. The person-centered counseling technique appears in many cases to be a necessary tool of the effective correctional counselor (Lester and Braswell, 109-110).

BEHAVIORISM OR LEARNING THEORY

Traditional Behaviorism

Counselors from the traditional behaviorist school of counseling appear least likely to acknowledge the truth of my thesis. One such behaviorist, B. F. Skinner, is in fact famous for making the claim that there is no such thing as human freedom. Nevertheless, full consideration of the practical requirements of traditional behaviorism will show that even the traditional behaviorists are at least implicitly interested in promoting freedom in their clients. It may, of course, be said that traditional behaviorist counseling is not truly correctional counseling by my definition in that the technique does not require a relationship to exist between a counselor and a client but only the provision of conditioning. In that case traditional behaviorism is no counterexample to my claim. By the fact, however, that a number of persons involved in correctional counseling employ a traditional behaviorist technique and have a traditional behaviorist orientation, it is important to consider their point of view.

Traditional behaviorist counseling is a technique that is sometimes referred to as behavior modification. It is a technique derived from Learning or Stimulus-Response theory. This theory holds that all behavior is learned, whether deviant or normal, and all behavior can be

unlearned. It is unconcerned with rationality, emotional states, or subjective experience and consequently is considered to be directly at
odds with other theories in its sole focus on behavior. It posits two basic types of learning—classical and operant conditioning.

In classical conditioning an unconditioned stimulus is paired with
neutral stimuli repeatedly until the formerly neutral stimuli alone produces the response normally only elicited by the unconditioned stimulus. Pavlov's dogs salivating at the sound of a bell is the classic example of this form of conditioning. For the traditional behaviorist,
classical conditioning is the means by which persons develop con-
sciences. By repeatedly pairing punishment and pain with "bad" behavior, the child eventually feels anticipatory pain and anxiety when
thinking about committing a "bad" act, which serves to make the
child refrain from it. From the traditional behaviorist viewpoint,
someone with no conscience has failed to classically condition appropriately.

With operant conditioning, the response to a stimulus is reinforced,
which makes the response more likely to recur whenever the stimulus
occurs. For example, if the only way a child can get his parents' attention is to misbehave, then he learns to misbehave in order to get
their attention. The stimulus is a situation in which the child feels anx-
ious due to being ignored, the response is bad behavior, and the reinforcement is parental attention, which reduces the child's anxiety. In
this sort of case, parents unintentionally shape the child's behavior
through operant conditioning. Reinforcers can be either positive or
negative. In the case just mentioned, the reinforcer is negative because it reduces anxiety or offsets an unpleasant stimulus. Positive reinforcement, on the other hand, is the onset of a pleasant stimulus
(i.e., it increases pleasure). Skinner, for one, prefers the use of only
positive reinforcement as a more humane tool of the therapist, such as
giving food, drink, or affection to promote the recurrence of valued
behavior.

The sort of treatment dictated by learning theory is conceptualized
as relearning or retraining. Behavioral problems are conceived as the
products of faulty learning or inappropriate classical or operant conditioning. These two forms of conditioning have some similarities in
that the unconditioned stimulus in classical conditioning may be
viewed as reinforcing the association between the conditioned stimu-

lus and the response, and in that the reinforced response in operant conditioning seems to become paired or associated with the stimulus that precedes it. The principal difference is that in operant conditioning the response elicited is an instrumental one, while in classical conditioning the response is noninstrumental.

To defend my claim that self-determination is on the implicit agenda of the traditional behaviorist counselor, I think it worthwhile to consider these two forms of conditioning separately as they have actually been used by traditional behaviorists working with offenders.

Classical Conditioning

Classical conditioning of persons with offending behaviors is described as aversive. That is, a neutral stimulus is paired with a stimulus that produces certain negative responses so that the neutral stimulus produces these same responses. The point is to make persons afraid of or upset by objects that once attracted them. A miniphobia is created. For instance, therapists have injected alcoholics with apomorphine, waited until the drug was about to make them feel nauseated, and then given them a shot of alcohol to drink. The alcoholic subsequently drinks and vomits. This procedure is repeated until the alcoholic starts to vomit at even the sight, smell, or thought of alcohol. The same sort of procedure has been used with sexual offenders by pairing the preferred sexual object with nausea. Besides drugs, other aversive conditioners that have been used include electric shock that clients can administer themselves and covert sensitization in which the therapist creates a fantasy for the client in which nauseating elements are woven into a story involving the desired object. Clients can use a tape-recording of the story to condition themselves at home.

While this technique is generally quite effective on a temporary basis, it can only work to promote significant long-term change if certain conditions are met. First, the client has to be motivated to change his behavior. It is easy to undo the effects of aversive conditioning. All the alcoholic has to do to extinguish (eliminate) his negative response to alcohol is to get drunk several times after the drug treatment has been suspended. In *A Clockwork Orange,* Alex could have extinguished what he had learned by simply getting into a few fights. He had no need to kill himself. Second, the client must not only be moti-vated to avoid alcohol, he must also have the opportunity to learn some new socially appropriate behavior as an alternative to the de-viant behavior. For instance, if he has been inclined to drink in times of stress, he must learn other means of stress reduction. If he has been inclined to fight when facing conflicts with others, he must learn other means of conflict resolution.

Since traditional behaviorists, like other counselors, are interested in long-term change, they must be concerned with promoting the de-sire for change in their clients. Harry Frankfurt refers to this sort of desire, the desire to change one's desires, as a second-order desire. Frankfurt has claimed that the existence of second-order desires is ev-idence of human freedom (1971). Other philosophers have questioned the sufficiency of second-order desires for freedom (e.g., see Slote, 1980), but I believe that a case can be made for their necessity. If we consider that in the prereflective consciousness the child can only be-gin to develop an object-self after she has internalized the prohibition of the parent, which is a desire that conflicts with her natural im-pulses, and a developed object-self is a necessary prerequisite for self-determination, then it seems clear that the presence of second-order desires are necessary. The presence of these desires thus do not guar-antee freedom but are a necessary stage on the road to freedom. The traditional behaviorist must certainly acknowledge the presence of these second-order desires and promote them if he is to succeed in his work. In promoting these desires (perhaps through positive reinforce-ment) in order to advance the client's capacity for self-control, he is in fact furthering the client's advance toward self-determination as well.

The traditional behaviorist can claim that second-order desires are the same as first-order desires in being the product of conditioning. That is, she can say that desires which conflict originate in response to different conditioning. While the alcoholic's desire for alcohol was originally reinforced by the pleasure he received from drinking, his desire to quit drinking was shaped by the pain he experienced from such things as the expressed displeasure of significant others at his drinking, loss of employment, and legal problems. Since the pain felt from these experiences may not override the pleasure associated with drinking, classical conditioning in this sort of case is intended to temporarily eliminate the pleasure associated with drinking so that it no longer impedes the desire to quit drinking. The traditional behaviorist can acknowledge that the desire to quit drinking must also be present for classical conditioning to work.

The difficulty with this explanation, however, is that it does not adequately address the complexities of human behavior. The pleasure the alcoholic derives from drinking is quite intense. It is so intense that many alcoholics are reluctant to relinquish it even in the face of very painful consequences involving social and occupational difficulties or the effect of nausea. The fact that many alcoholics do strive to stop drinking even though the immediate pleasure of drinking may seem to them to outweigh the immediate and long-term pain that drinking causes them confounds the traditional behaviorist explanation. The traditional behaviorist cannot explain why reducing pain should be more attractive than seeking pleasure. He simply sees persons as acting to promote pleasure and to reduce pain. Pleasure and pain are for him simple constructs which do not admit qualitative differences, because he acknowledges no essential human traits, such as sociality or rationality. The traditional behaviorist needs to be able to explain why the second-order desire not to drink is a *better* desire than the first-order desire to drink, but he cannot.

Consequently, traditional behaviorists who successfully classically condition must at least implicitly rely on the possibility of human freedom, even when they do not recognize its existence. For classical conditioning to work in the long-term, the client must see its purpose as meeting his needs as a social and rational individual. The client must see his second-order desire as a *better* desire because it meets his human needs, which override his momentary needs. In having this evaluative capacity and acting on it, the client evidences his freedom.

Operant Conditioning

Operant conditioning, the shaping of behavior through the positive reinforcement of appropriate behavior, has been used extensively with delinquents. Token economies, for instance, in which youths receive points for such things as academic achievement, has been a common practice in juvenile correctional institutions. Lester and

Braswell discuss a number of behavioral programs for delinquents in which operant conditioning is used to shape behavior (136-143).

Particular instances of such conditioning include attempts to decrease misbehavior through paying attention to a child when she does something desirable. Providing instruction to help the child acquire social, academic, and vocational skills is intended to help her learn how to obtain rewards through legitimate means. Teaching the child such skills as how to get and keep jobs is intended to help her learn essential controls for her behavior. Behavioral contracts are sometimes used between parents and children in order to ease friction at home and provide a living environment less likely to reinforce negative behaviors.

These techniques are certainly not incompatible with the methods of other theories. In fact, in many cases the behaviorists who employ them use a counseling style not unlike counselors with different theoretical orientations. The basic difference seems to be a matter of explanation. The traditional behaviorists simply see the counselor reinforcing certain statements the client makes and focusing on some issues rather than others and thereby shaping the client's behavior. It is of interest that Lester and Braswell find one study in which it was observed that behaviorist counselors interacted with their clients with higher levels of empathy and interpersonal contact than ordinary counselors (143). It seems that these behaviorists are achieving the sort of counseling relationship endorsed by Rogers for facilitating change.

In the case of delinquent youth, it appears that the purpose of operant conditioning is to instill the desire to behave in a socially appropriate way. Unlike classical conditioning, there is no need to presume an initial desire for change. Rather, appropriate behavior is reinforced by the operant conditioner through food, tokens for various privileges, or empathic responses in a counseling interaction. The effect of this last reinforcer seems to be a closer identification with the counselor who is both an authority figure and a role model to the youthful client. This is the view of Albert Bandura, who advocates a more moderate, or less externally determined view, of behaviorism in his social learning theory. Bandura rejects Skinner's view of humans as organisms manipulated by external stimuli by claiming that learning can also be gained by observing the behavior of others and its consequences. In making this claim, Bandura opens the door for socially mediated experience, which I have argued is an important basis for advances in self-determination.

If Skinner is correct, it would appear that the pleasure of such rewards as food and tokens would be as capable of eliciting positive behavioral change in delinquents as the reward of empathic concern. Whether this is so is difficult to ascertain from the correctional research because it appears that juvenile correctional institutions generally are interested in promoting positive relationships between staff and inmates. Skinner's reductionistic view of human behavior may, therefore, never be clearly substantiated in the correctional setting.

Insofar as many of the successful behaviorists are involved in empathic relationships with their delinquent clients, it does seem possible that the empathic relationship is a necessary positive reinforcer of socially appropriate behavior. If it is necessary, it may well be because this relationship, albeit meant only to condition, actually promotes identification of the youth with the counselor. In identifying with the counselor, the youth begins to see things from another perspective and is consequently increasingly able to determine which of his impulses are the best to follow. So, by this interpretation, even the traditional behaviorist correctional counselor promotes self-determination (albeit unknowingly) insofar as she empathizes with her client. For the traditional behaviorist correctional counselor to achieve long-term success with her client, I think that this must be the case. Otherwise, there would be little reason for the juvenile to maintain her good behavior after release, particularly when she returns to an environment which is likely to reinforce bad behavior.

To clarify this point, consider the case of a young man who tends to fight whenever he feels threatened. A behaviorist counselor in a correctional institution may treat this behavior by reinforcing an alternative response such as walking away through giving the youth tokens or patting him on the back whenever he walks away from a threatening situation. Clearly, the behaviorist counselor hopes that the youth will generalize this response to any situation in which he feels threatened, whether in the institution or in the community. However, there is no assurance that he will because he has only learned to walk away in response to a situation-specific stimulus (i.e., one that occurs within the institution). According to research, this sort of behaviorist technique appears to improve institutional adjustment. However, as Carney observes, there does not seem to be a basis for believing that this technique in itself creates long-term changes in behavior (121).

For significant long-term change to occur, it is imperative for the youth to be able to generalize his socially appropriate responses to situations outside of the institution where there may be no possibility of consistent reinforcement. To do this, he must begin to internalize the perspective of others. The establishment of an empathic relationship with a counselor is a first step, and it is an important means toward the goal of self-determination. In identifying with another who values socially appropriate responses, the youth begins to make the other's values and responses his own.

Contemporary Behaviorism—
Social Learning and Cognitive Therapy

Inspired by the work of Bandura and Aaron Beck, many contemporary behaviorists address the above specified deficiencies of the traditional behaviorist explanations of offender behavior by acknowledging the importance of vicarious learning and cognitive processes in shaping behavior. In this section I discuss Bandura's work with offenders and several other cognitivist-behaviorist techniques for modifying criminal behavior. The cognitivist group resembles rational theory (which will be discussed in the next section) in focusing on client beliefs. However, the cognitivists deny that all psychopathology has a similar set of underlying irrational beliefs, which rational theories claim. The cognitivists believe that each psychological disorder has its own unique cognitive content and that problematic beliefs are maladaptive and interfere with normal cognitive processing. They operate from an inductive model in which clients are helped to translate interpretations and beliefs into hypotheses, which are then subjected to empirical testing.

Bandura's social learning theory claims that most human learning occurs through a process of observational learning. That is, persons chiefly learn vicariously by observing the consequences of other persons' behavior, and they tend to model those others who are viewed as attractive, competent, and rewarded for their behavior. Persons also tend to be discouraged from behavior they see others being punished for. The theory attributes criminal behavior to vicarious learning from antisocial associates or role models. In its focus on observation, cognitive processing is viewed as essential. For Bandura, much of human learning involves the cognitions that prompt and support behavior or appraise the stimuli presented. Consequently, the effectiveness of all environmental factors (including role models) depends on how the client perceives and cognitively organizes these factors. In its concern with perceptions, it shares some insights with phenomenological theory.

The correctional counselor practicing Bandura's method of observational learning functions essentially as a role model of prosocial behavior that reinforces and encourages the practice on the part of the client of new positive behaviors. Reinforcement often involves praise for positive actions and expressions of disapproval for bad behavior, which are followed by suggestions for alternative positive behaviors. Throughout the process, it is essential for the counselor to be consistent and clear in his modeling and reinforcement.

Some social learning programs are referred to as forms of skill training. Since many offenders are deficient in social skills, prosocial modeling by counselors and other correctional staff is used in these programs to help the offenders acquire new social skills. Some programs recognize the difficulty of having offenders generalize these skills to their home environments and try to promote generalization through helping their clients "overlearn" their skills, role play using the skills in stressful situations, or work with the family to encourage them to reinforce the new skills.

In Ross and Fabiano's Cognitive Skills and Living Skills program, there is a strong emphasis on the claim that offenders have not acquired the cognitive skills needed for effective social adaptation. This program attempts to teach offenders such skills as self-control, the ability to take the perspective of the other, problem solving, formulating short-term and long-term plans, avoiding high-risk situations, anticipating the consequences of one's behavior, and decision making. Clients are trained to focus on thinking patterns that lead to criminal activity, and role playing is used as a means to explore alternative responses to stressful situations.

Kohlberg's moral education theory has also inspired some treatment strategies with offenders that seem fit into the cognitivist-behaviorist classification because of their focus on improving cognitive structures as a means of improving behavior. The aim of such strategies is to help offenders achieve growth to the third stage of moral judgment, where prosocial and empathic orientations begin. Kohlberg claims that exposure to fair and participatory environments promotes moral development. In his own work with inmate offenders, Kohlberg encouraged the use of discussions about moral dilemmas and offering inmates some responsibility for making decisions in the governance of their own living units.

Yet another technique of the cognitivist-behaviorists is Anger Control Training (ACT). ACT teaches delinquent, aggressive, and conduct-disordered youth to identify and deal with the sources of their anger through a five-step process. The youths are taught to identify trigger situations, to recognize physiological clues of anger, to create "self-statements" as a means of lowering anger arousal (e.g., telling oneself to calm down), to reduce anger by stress reduction techniques, and to self-evaluate their progress in controlling anger.

With all of the aforementioned cognitivist-behaviorist theories and techniques, there is a clear interest in the self-determination of the offender-client. It is thus not surprising that Kohlberg's theory can be found here. The cognitivist-behaviorists are interested in improving the cognitive skills of the client and in improving her capacity for internalizing new perspectives, in particular a prosocial one. They each value a prosocial orientation as most adaptive and thus are able to explain, unlike the behaviorist who classically conditions, why therapeutic improvements are truly of benefit to the client. Further, in helping the client internalize a new prosocial orientation, they pave the way for clients to generalize their learning to new situations in which the possibility of positive reinforcement for good behavior is negligible. Thus, they have a great advantage over the behaviorist who strictly uses operant conditioning.

RATIONAL APPROACHES—
ELLIS, GLASSER, GREENWALD

The rational approach to psychological impairment focuses on thinking processes. It attributes psychological and behavioral problems to irrational and irresponsible thinking. It aspires to increase rationality and responsibility and constructive problem solving in clients. It differs from the cognitivist theory described in the last section in addressing psychological problems with a deductive-philosophical approach. The most notable rationalist psychotherapists are Albert Ellis, who is responsible for Rational-Emotive Behavior Therapy, and William Glasser, who is known for Reality Therapy. H. Greenwald, who developed Direct Decision Therapy, is less well known. All three have used their rational technique in working with offenders. In promoting rationality and responsibility, all three are interested in making clients more realistic. In doing so, they are also interested in making them increasingly self-determined.

There are some interesting variations in these three theories and techniques. However, in spite of their differences, I argue that each is interested in promoting self-determination.

Ellis

Ellis believes that psychological problems are caused by emotional states that result from irrational beliefs. For Ellis, irrational beliefs decrease happiness and maximize pain, while rational beliefs increase happiness and minimize pain. This is because rational beliefs are realistic. Irrational beliefs, on the other hand, are related to unrealistic and empirically invalid hypotheses that prevent persons from fulfilling their desires. Rational-emotive counseling teaches clients that debilitating emotional states are entirely a result of irrational beliefs. They learn in counseling to dispute these beliefs and to replace them with rational beliefs that make them happier and able to make more appropriate decisions.

Ellis hypothesizes that in many cases the psychopathic bravado of offenders disguises low self-esteem. In working with these persons, Ellis shows them, in a noncritical manner, the self-defeating pattern of their criminal activity. He believes it is important for them to realize that their offending behavior has harmed them. This bravado may disguise the offender's irrational belief that he is a loser and has no socially appropriate means of succeeding in life. Consequently, he flaunts societal rules by engaging in offenses that only serve to alienate him from other persons who could help foster the positive capabilities he does have.

Yockelson and Samenow developed a program that has been used in at least two correctional settings that appears to be a direct descendant of Ellis' theory. In their program, they target and seek to correct irrational, erroneous, and faulty thinking in offenders. They believe that the thinking errors of offenders serve to support, excuse, and sometimes reinforce criminal behavior.

Glasser

Glasser attributes psychological problems to a person's inability to fulfill essential needs. He claims that the degree of severity of the psychological symptoms is directly related to what extent these essential needs are not being met. When persons are unsuccessful in fulfilling them, Glasser says it is chiefly because they deny reality in the world. The goal of Glasser's Reality Therapy is to teach clients to recognize and accept reality and to try to fulfill their needs within the framework of reality.

Glasser believes there are two basic human needs—the need to love and be loved and the need to feel we are worthwhile to ourselves and to others. Consequently, he says that persons must involve themselves with at least one other person and maintain a conventionally satisfactory standard of behavior. Being psychologically well-adjusted means that a person upholds and respects the rules of conventional morality. It means that she must not deprive others of the ability to fulfill their needs when she fulfills her own. In doing so, she is responsible. If she fails in this endeavor, she is irresponsible. The counselor promotes responsible behavior and discourages irresponsible behavior.

Glasser says that young offenders suffer a universal malady. They are unwilling to take responsibility for the consequences of their behavior to themselves and to their community. The counselor who does Reality Therapy with offenders is quite confrontive with her frequently manipulative clients in order to teach them to take responsibility for their actions. At the same time Glasser believes the counselor should transiently fulfill the client's need for a loving relationship. The counseling relationship thus serves to supply the "essential person" who has a strong concern for the client until the time when the client can find that "essential person" in others.

Greenwald

Greenwald specifically addresses the decisions people make in his Direct-Decision Therapy. He sees all psychological problems, including characterological ones, as the result of decisions people have made. Counseling commences with discovering the context in which these were made. Once it is discovered, Greenwald claims the client will realize that his decision was not rational. In arriving at this point the counselor focuses on the payoffs of the original decision as a means of motivating the client to make the decision to change his present behavior. The counselor also helps him weigh the costs of alternative decisions, but the client is expected to do most of the work. If the client realizes the cost of his original decision is too great, then the counselor helps him carry through his new decision and continually reaffirms his choice. In this process, Greenwald believes that the counselor must be empathetic and authentic (like the person-centered counselor). The main goal is always awareness of the choice that has been made and its consequences in relation to other possible choices.

Differences and Commonalities

While Ellis, Glasser, and Greenwald share the belief that counseling is intended to make the client more rational and realistic, there are some interesting differences in their theories. First, unlike the other two, Ellis does not believe that the counselor must be empathic and genuine for therapeutic change to occur. In his view, it may be desirable for a Rogerian-style relationship to exist between the counselor and client, but he doubts that Rogers' conditions are necessary or sufficient for therapeutic change. In some cases, he thinks that merely pointing out the self-defeating consequences of a person's behavior and suggesting alternative behaviors is sufficient. Also, a person-centered counselor may be disinclined to be sufficiently confrontive to enable the client to see how his behavior is self-defeating. (For many correctional counselors working with highly manipulative offenders, this last concern is a real worry about Rogers' approach.)

Second, Glasser differs from Ellis and Greenwald in viewing the counselor as a moralist. Since Glasser believes that maladjustment occurs whenever conventional morality is flouted, he believes it is

necessary for the counselor to promote conventional moral standards. This view has subjected Glasser to some criticism because, for
instance, he considers homosexual behavior irresponsible. Reality
Therapy, as Lester and Braswell observe, presupposes a system of
morality that we all agree on. Clearly, there is much disagreement
about the immorality of homosexuality. Contrary to Glasser, Greenwald insists that to be effective the counselor must be nonjudgmen-
tal in moral matters. He thinks that the counselor's principal duty is
to help the client perceive the payoffs of his decisions. Thus, only if
the consequence of the decision to engage in homosexual activity involves social ostracism (a doubtful consequence in our society) and
the client decides that being ostracized is a worse consequence than
that predicted to follow from not engaging in this behavior would
counseling tend to discourage it. Yet in that case it would be the
client's decision to change his behavior, not the counselor's. As for
Ellis, he assumes that offending behavior is self-defeating, but he
does not make any presuppositions about essential human need in
making this claim. Rather, he simply seems to assume that persons
who offend irrationally limit their choices of behavior due to a negative self-evaluation. Their choices are irrational because they do not
realize their full capacities and not because they have an essential
need to fulfill them.

On the other hand, Lester and Braswell worry that there is a danger
that counselors from any of these rational orientations may merely in-
doctrinate rather than truly benefit their clients. They wonder, "Who
defines what is irrational?" (128). They discuss the case of a woman
involved in violent sexual activity whose desires for this activity related to her religious convictions. Her counselor treated her by attacking her religious beliefs as irrational. Unfortunately, they do not
specify which of the woman's religious beliefs were attacked. I think
rational people would agree that the religious beliefs of the followers
of Jim Jones that required them to follow him into mass suicide were
irrational. If some of the woman's religious beliefs were directly responsible for her self-destructive behavior, then it is appropriate for
the counselor to attack them. Attacking those specific irrational beliefs, however, should not necessarily undermine her other and more
basic religious beliefs unless she follows the creed of a dangerous
cult. Further, such cults are often offshoots of mainstream religions,

which do not typically endorse self-destructive behavior. Thus, a person could rationally reject the self-endangering beliefs of the cult without abandoning her more rational religious beliefs.

Consequently, there is a substantial difference in dogmatism between Glasser, Greenwald, and Ellis. The latter two seem to presuppose a conception of rationality that is more generally accepted. Glasser, of course, posits a social view of human nature and essential human need that is consistent with my previous discussion of the need for mutual recognition. In his aspirations for counseling, Glasser appears to be quite interested in advancing clients' capacities for self-determination. Like Rogers, Glasser wants clients to make significant improvements in being self- and other-regarding. Thus, he also affirms the importance of unconditional positive regard in the counseling relationship as a means for promoting self-esteem and responsible behavior. He also wants the client to feel positively about the authority figure of the counselor. Through that close connection, the client becomes capable of comprehending and appreciating the perspective of authority and internalizing its values.

While Ellis does not think such regard is necessary for therapeutic change to occur in the counseling relationship, his conception of rationality (and that of Greenwald's) is compatible with mine. In this compatibility we find that Ellis and Greenwald are similarly interested in promoting the self-determination of clients in consequence of their interest in promoting rationality. In the last chapter I argued that improvements in self-determination reflect improvements in rationality. A person becomes increasingly rational as she more fully understands the consequences of her decisions. She understands these consequences more fully by comprehending the perspective of other persons. This comprehension allows her to understand when others are likely to thwart her goals by punishing her, and it allows her a greater understanding of the real world, its limits, and its potentialities for action. In their concern with making clients more realistic, therefore, Ellis and Greenwald do care about enhancing self-determination. Without such knowledge, little possibility for growth and true autonomy is possible.

* * *

In sum, all four of the primary theoretical orientations endorsed by persons involved in correctional counseling have an explicit (or implicit, in the case of the behaviorists) interest in promoting self-determination in their offender-clients. It can be reasonably asserted that any psychological perspective on the origins of offender behavior arises from one of these four orientations. Enhancing self-determination does matter. From the perspective of the moral education theorist, it certainly should matter if punishment in any particular case can be justified.

Chapter Six

Concluding Remarks

There remain a few points that deserve clarification in concluding this work. These pertain to the descriptive nature of the claim that self-determination is a goal of correctional counseling, Kratcoski's belief that correctional counseling has as its primary end the benefit of society, and why the differing conceptions of self-determination described as goals of the four psychological therapeutic orientations are truly consistent with each other. Robert B. Redmon and Joseph Margolis separately argue for conceptions of the nature and goals of psychiatry, which may generate doubt about some of my claims. As correctional counseling is sometimes performed by psychiatrists as well as other mental health professionals, their arguments are worth considering. They also bring into question Brace's broader claim—that self-determination is a nonrelativistic goal of psychotherapy, since psychotherapy and counseling are roughly equivalent terms and are the genus under which correctional counseling and much of psychiatry falls.

REDMON'S OBJECTION

In critiquing Robert Lipkin's claim that the psychiatrist is a moral advisor, Redmon argues that "the question of what psychiatry *is*, is a question of what it *ought* to be" (332). He believes that psychiatry (and, by implication, correctional counseling performed by psychiatrists) is necessarily a normative concept because when persons choose to make use of psychiatrists, they already have certain expectations about what psychiatry should do for them. He notes that Plato and Hippocrates believed that the professions are essentially known by their ends and that these ends entail certain moral responsibilities. He argues that the difficulty with this long-held belief is that definitions in themselves do not entail moral principles because morality does not follow from facts alone, and the Platonic view leads to vacuous definitions of the professions. Rather, he says that when the history or current codes of a profession are relevant to its present ends, it is only because the history or codes lead to expectations or to a promise which clients can reasonably expect to have fulfilled.

In defining correctional counseling, I stated that it always involves a relationship between two persons, a convicted offender who needs and desires (or can desire) assistance with a specific problem, and a helping professional who wishes to facilitate change in the offender and who has knowledge of at least one psychological theory and associated treatment modality. I argued that the provision of this activity entails an interest by the counselor in promoting the self-determination of the offender. If the relationship as described does not exist, then counseling is not occurring. Certainly, the offender who wants help expects the counselor to want to help him. However, this expectation alone does not make my claim a normative one. This is because the offender expects much more from the counselor. He wants the counselor to have a *correct* understanding of the source of his problem and knowledge of the *correct* treatment modality that will resolve his problem. My definition allows for the possibility that the counselor may have false beliefs about the source of the offender's problem and the appropriate means for correcting it. In such a case, counseling is occurring, but it is not likely to be effective. Clients reasonably expect that counseling be effective in addressing their problems when they consent to undertake it.

My definition does incorporate an end and a professional responsibility in including the requirements of interest and particular knowledge. However, these ends do not entail a specifically moral responsibility because they do not speak to the offender's desire for a successful outcome. Having an interest in promoting change cannot by itself make change occur. More specifically, having an interest in promoting self-determination does not guarantee that self-determination will be promoted. A person should also have a correct understanding of what change, and specifically self-determination, requires. Thus, while my definition incorporates an end, it may be regarded as omitting a final end, which was important to the conceptions of the professions discussed by Plato and Hippocrates. In this important omission, my definition of correctional counseling and my claim about what it entails can be correctly regarded as descriptive.

It may be objected that there are some correctional counselors who have no desire to help their offender clients. Recall my discussion of the concept of correctional counseling in chapter 5. It is neither necessary nor sufficient to have the title of "correctional counselor" in order to be a person involved in correctional counseling. Consequently, my descriptive claim cannot be either validated or disproved by polling all persons employed as "correctional counselors." My description was derived from closely considering the definitions of counseling and correctional counseling provided by the American Psychological Association and the American Correctional Association as well as important texts in the field. It can be fairly assumed that the professional associations represent a general consensus of persons working in these fields when they arrive at definitions designed to describe their professional activity. These associations, of course, are also concerned with establishing ethical codes for the proper conduct of professionals. The codes represent the normative aims of the profession in spelling out how persons engaged in the professional activity in question should function. Thus, it is important for them to commence with a definition that is purely descriptive in order to demarcate the area of activity which needs to be professionally regulated. While the codes lead to certain expectations, the description of the sorts of activities to which they apply do not. Correctional counseling as I describe it entails knowledge of at least one psychological theory regarding the cause and treatment of offending behavior, but I provide no assurance in my account that the knowledge is correct or that it is correctly applied. A normative account would provide some assurance.

Redmon is intent on defeating Lipkin's claim because he worries that if Lipkin is believed to be correct that moral problems will become "medicalized" and offenders will be treated rather than punished. In previous chapters I argued that counseling with offenders can promote self-determination and that advances in self-determination parallel improvements in moral judgment, which may lead to improvements in moral behavior. As I describe it, counseling is not medical treatment because it does not treat persons as mere physical objects, which traditional medical treatment tends to do.

I agree with Redmon, when he also argues contra Lipkin, that in most cases psychiatry only gives prudential advice. However, as I have shown in the discussion of Kohlberg's hierarchy of moral judgment, persons who make advances in prudential judgment or instrumental rationality are making moral advances. So, when the psychiatrist or correctional counselor promotes prudentiality in her client by giving prudential advice, she is also learning to be a better moral judge and possibly a better moral actor as well.

MARGOLIS' OBJECTION

Margolis maintains that psychiatry has a strong ideological dimension and there is no proof that its goals have a nonconventional basis. If Margolis is correct and psychiatry has no purely objective goals, then it would appear that Kratcoski may also be correct in claiming that society always sets the standards for correctional treatment, which will chiefly be to satisfy its own interests. In that case, the self-determination of the offender-client would only be a secondary and possibly dispensable goal of correctional counseling. Consequently, Margolis' argument is well worth answering.

Margolis commences with an examination of Arman Nicholi's (editor-in-chief of *The Harvard Guide to Modern Psychiatry*) claim about the nature of the psychiatrist-patient relationship. Nicholi says that this relationship exists in order to evaluate and treat the conflicts prompting the patient to seek psychiatric help and that it focuses solely on the needs of the patient. Margolis zeroes in on Nicholi's use of the word "conflicts" to argue, like Redmon, that this claim based on the Hippocratic precepts is subject to the standard counterargument. That is, if the relationship is a professional one, "then the code of conduct and proper function of psychiatrists *cannot but reflect an entire society's reasoned view of the service that profession is to provide*" (174). From this relativistic perspective, Margolis claims that even benefiting the sick is derived and authorized from a larger notion of social well-being, which is always open to revision in the name of that interest. Margolis argues that certain conceptual puzzles regarding the nature of the conflicts Nicholi refers to involve both the social responsibilities of psychiatrists and the distinctive nature of the range of psychiatric complaints and that while these issues are distinct they are effectively inseparable. Thus, Margolis claims that an ineliminable feature of psychiatry is its strong ideological dimension (Margolis, 173-175).

Margolis claims that while purely somatic medicine attempts to achieve objectivity in its ends by referring to what is necessary to the functioning of *homo sapiens*, psychiatry cannot achieve this objectivity because its focus is not on *homo sapiens* per se, but rather its focus in treatment is on the norms of the human person. Different cultures have varying conceptions of personhood and its value. Due to the culturally relative norms of personhood, the norms of psychiatry cannot escape being conventionally dictated.

In his argument, Margolis suggests that the best attempt to define mental disorder, or the problem that psychiatry is meant to correct, in a nonrelativistic sense comes from Culver and Gert in their definition of malady. They define malady as follows: A person has a malady if and only if he has a condition, other than his rational beliefs and desires, such that he is suffering, or at a significantly increased risk of suffering, a nontrivial harm or evil (death, pain, disability, loss of freedom or opportunity, or loss of pleasure) in the absence of a distinct sustaining cause.[1]

They hold that the fact that persons in all cultures deplore the five specified evils gives their account objectivity. As long as psychiatry is acting to alleviate one or more of these evils, they believe that it has universal ends. While this account may seem initially plausible, Margolis proceeds to prove that it has problems as well. In this section, I argue that Margolis is correct in his reasons for defeating Culver and Gert's account, yet I show that his claim regarding the relativistic nature of psychiatric goals can be defeated by consideration of my previous arguments, particularly those regarding distinctions in low and high levels of autonomy.

Margolis says that "the telltale slippage" of the Culver and Gert account is revealed in the following argument. First, Culver and Gert distinguish disorders of the body from disorders of persons. That is, disorders of persons are not restricted to dysfunction of organs. Second, they say that both physical and mental maladies are maladies of persons. (It seems that we are first persons and only derivatively members of the species *homo sapiens*.) Third, they define a disability (one of the evils) as the lack of an ability that is characteristic of the species. Fourth, they fail to notice that even if there are abilities characteristic of *homo sapiens*, it does not follow that there are comparably clear abilities characteristic of all human persons. Since what is valued in terms of the functioning of persons varies between cultures, what counts as a disability is culturally inconsistent. Margolis maintains that they do not clearly distinguish the functions of culturally developed persons, whose longevity, for instance, may be impacted by advances in science and technology, from the behavioral or holistic functions of mere members of a biologic species. The main problem, however, is that "the selection of statistical patterns [i.e., what is characteristic] is itself a form of normative preference *as well as* one that inevitably depends on culturally favored values not reducible to the species-specific" (179).

In the preceding argument, Margolis focuses on the relativistic nature of disability in persons, which is only one of the five evils. Most persons would regard death as the worst, but on the subject of death, Margolis points out that Culver and Gert again run into problems. This is because Culver and Gert regard suicide as a malady unless a rational ordering of evils would show it to be a lesser evil than, for instance, pain. At this point they run into a ranking problem. Recall my worry about the circularity of their account in chapter 3. They justify paternalistic actions toward persons who have irrational desires, which they define as having no adequate reason for desiring to suffer an evil. A reason is inadequate on their account "if any significant group of otherwise rational people regard the harm avoided or benefit gained as at least as important as the harm suffered" (Culver and Gert, 1997, 28).

As Margolis suggests, rationality on this account cannot help but be subservient to the culture's standards for rational behavior. This point is more apparent in consideration of Culver and Gert's own example. They refer to Jehovah's Witnesses refusing blood transfusions due to their religious beliefs. According to Culver and Gert, these persons are not irrational because they believe that no rankings of evils held by any significant religious, national, or cultural group count as irrational, and because psychiatrists generally respect these sorts of beliefs. They do not, however, clearly specify what they mean by "significant." In our American culture where freedom of religion is respected, there seems to be no difficulty with counting the Jehovah's Witness' refusal of blood transfusions as rational. On the other hand, religious cults such as that of Jim Jones are generally considered irrational when the members engage in mass suicide. Culver and Gert seem able to explain this difference in respect for religious belief because the Jim Jones group was not very significant, at least in terms of numbers.

If we were to consider the case of the Jehovah's Witness in a different culture, it is not clear that we would get the same result. For instance, in the old Soviet culture where the fruits of science and technology were highly valued and religious freedom was devalued, it seems likely that the refusal of the Jehovah's Witness would have been regarded as irrational. Even with the possibility of significant (i.e., large) numbers of Jehovah's Witnesses living in the old Soviet Union, the standards of that particular culture for rational behavior would directly conflict with the beliefs of the Jehovah's Witness. The Soviets would see no distinction between this action and the actions of Jim Jones' followers because their culture gives no credence to religious beliefs of any kind.

As Margolis observes regarding the case of suicide, the distance between interventions to prevent it and the political use of psychiatry is not easy to establish. Competing views of "prudential evils" between cultures would justify competing views of paternalistic intervention and of the sort of mental health services "correctly" rendered by the psychiatrist in different societies (Margolis, 180). Hence, Culver and Gert's conceptions of malady and rationality are vulnerable to the charge of cultural relativism. I believe they are vulnerable chiefly because they do not consider why any harm is a harm to human beings as such. They do not provide a substantive account of what humans need.

In the course of this work, I believe I have answered Margolis' claim that psychiatry has only culturally determined ends. This is because I have argued that persons, by virtue of being members of the species *homo sapiens,* have certain universal needs. As humans, they need to be members of the moral community, which requires at a minimum having the desire to take only moral means to one's ends. Associated with this need is the need to be respected by others as a rational being, which requires having the capacity to not act on immoral desires. In the first chapter, I defended these needs by arguing that humans are essentially social animals who will isolate or ostracize any other humans who cannot or will not act in a minimally moral fashion. In the second chapter, I offered a more fully developed argument from Rawls to defend the existence of these needs. For Rawls, there is a basic human desire to utilize and maximize all of our talents, and our greatest and most complex talent is our capacity to acquire objective interests. In fulfilling this talent, Rawls believes humans most fully express their freedom and rationality. I think he is correct, though he leaves unexplained the basis for assuming that such a desire exists.

In the course of describing the levels of autonomy in chapters 3 and 4, I provided a basis for accepting the reality of this desire. Recall my description of Aboulafia's four stages on the road to self-determination, which are the prereflective consciousness, the prereflective sense of self, the reflective sense of self, and the final stage of self-determination. These stages parallel development along Kohlberg's hierarchy of moral judgment between at least Kohlberg stages one through three. The need to advance through these stages is not merely based on some innate need for self-definition, but it also (and possibly chiefly) rests on the need for improvement in the capacity to understand, make sense of, and be less vulnerable to the world humans find themselves in. Consequently, it can be said that the desire to flourish through the full exercise of talents, which Rawls posits, is ultimately grounded on a more basic desire for increasing empowerment in a world that at the least rational stages seems most unpredictable and most frightening.

Of course, it may be objected that I do not fully defend Rawls because Stage 2 of Kohlberg's hierarchy seems sufficient for prudence—the capacity to allay one's fears. But it is not. Only when a person begins to comprehend the perspective of a caring other and becomes involved in mutually caring relationships (at Stage 3) can a person's fears begin to be fully alleviated. This is because at Stage 3 a person realizes that she is not alone and that there really are other persons with whom she can ally herself in facing her fears because they value her ends as much as she does. There is no knowledge of caring at Stage 2.

Consequently, humans have a basic need to make advances in self-determination and all it entails. This is a need that transcends cultural differences. Consider the Jehovah's Witness case. Recall that Culver and Gert cannot explain why the Jehovah's Witness is rational in refusing treatment while the follower of Jim Jones is not in a culture that devalues religious freedom. Also recall my second criterion for justifying paternalistic intervention. A person may behave paternalistically only if the recipient has low autonomy desires or the recipient has high autonomy desires and would consent if she were fully informed about the consequences of intervention. It can be imagined that a Jehovah's Witness could have subjected the desires resulting from her religious beliefs to the sort of critical scrutiny described by Scoccia, but it seems highly unlikely that a follower of Jim Jones' cult would have done so. Part of our reason for making this distinction does not rest on the "significance" of one form of beliefs over another, but rather pertains to the legitimacy many persons find in the distinction of killing versus letting die. Active killing results in certain death, while letting die only results in probable death. Respecting the Jehovah's Witness' right to refuse treatment acknowledges the fact that medical science is imperfect and the outcome of any medical treatment always only probable. Refusing treatment is not suicide. Hence, the refusal of medical treatment by any adult with highly autonomous desires who is fully informed about the outcome of his refusal should be respected. On the other hand, the desire to commit suicide in any apparently healthy person whose desire has only low autonomy should probably not be. Paternalistic interventions, including those that involve psychiatric treatment or any form of counseling, should always aim to promote the development of autonomy whenever possible, and it must never interfere with well-informed high autonomy desires.

In the positive goal of self-determination we find a nonrelativistic end of any form of counseling. It is nonrelativistic because in any culture humans have the need to come to fully comprehend the perspective of others in their social environment so that they can understand their world and learn how to survive well in it. Granted, not every culture promotes advances in self-determination among its members, and in fact some try to promote dependency and to maintain persons of lower castes in narrow roles. I expect, however, that these cultures are least likely to survive and flourish in the long term because they make it unlikely for many persons within their cultures to have reason to truly accept conventional morality. Clearly, any culture must be interested in making its members accept its conventional morality. Thus, it must be interested in seeing its members make those advances in self-determination that bring them up to at least Stage 3 of Kohlberg's hierarchy. Further, for a culture to work really well, it will also be interested in seeing its members flourish in terms of advancing toward the postconventional stage so that they will be able to reform and improve the culture's moral standards. In consequence, regardless of the political idiosyncrasies of the culture within which correctional counseling takes place, it is also possible that persons involved in it can re-form and reconceive their theoretical perspective and techniques to better meet the universal human needs of their offender clientele.

THE DIFFERENCES IN THEORETICAL PERSPECTIVES

My aim in the last chapter was to show that each of the differing theoretical perspectives of correctional counseling is interested in promoting self-determination and that the conception of self-determination that each promotes is compatible with my own. Of course, these psychological theories are quite diverse in their explanation of human behavior and development. This may be due to significant differences in the philosophical traditions each theory follows. There are certainly substantial differences in emphasis on the importance of early childhood experience with important caregivers, cognitive functioning, emotional states, and external reinforcers of behavior. Because of this difference in emphasis and the development by each theory of its own unique jargon for describing maladaptive states and their remedies, it may seem unlikely that all could arrive at a consensus in regard to even one goal of counseling. Consequently, it may be objected that while each theory promotes self-determination, my conception of this goal of counseling is not fully inclusive of the disparate conceptions presented.

Against this objection, I argue here that my conception is fully inclusive. My claim, stated at the beginning of chapter 5, is that a person becomes increasingly self-determined as her cognitive and empathic capacities for perceiving herself from the role of the other and for perceiving herself as a person capable of changing into a new way of being improves. These two properties are described as necessary — though not sufficient — for advancing toward a self-determined state. Recall that the condition of mutual respect is also necessary. Each of the theories that I have examined is interested in at least promoting these first two necessary conditions.

The psychoanalytic counselor strives to help the delinquent internalize the counselor's own prohibitions and moral ideals in order for him to gain superego controls over his behavior. With the adult neurotic, she strives to strengthen her client's rational ego desires by bringing his id desires into conscious awareness in order to bring them under conscious and rational control. In both cases, the counselor aims toward self-governance and self-determination. In the first case, we clearly see an interest in an empathic advance in perceiving the self from the role of the other through the internalization of the counselor's ideals. Consequently, we also see an interest in having the client perceive himself as someone new, as someone who is now capable of restraining his id desires. In the second case, there is a strong interest in a cognitive advance through the recognition of formerly unconscious id desires. In this new self-understanding, the client has internalized the perceptions of his therapist and is thereby made capable of addressing his own problems. He is also now capable of seeing himself as a person who is more likely to get what he wants.

For the TA counselor, the offender is typically playing a self-defeating game. Like the psychoanalytic counselor, the TA counselor aims to bring this and other games to conscious awareness during the course of counseling. In this process, TA believes the offender will begin to be capable of achieving genuine and intimate relationships with others, which will be possible only insofar as he also internalizes moral values. Thus, TA wants the client to make cognitive advances in terms of perceiving communications from different perspectives and in internalizing those perspectives, and it is interested in having the client begin to see himself as a person capable of social control, which for TA is the capacity to end self-defeating games.

With Rogers' person-centered counseling, there is a greater emphasis on affective rather than cognitive development, but there remains a keen interest in having the client accept and fully internalize the empathic perceptions of the counselor. This counselor wants the client to perceive himself as unconditionally worthy, and thus she wants him to experience himself with the unconditional positive regard that the counselor feels for him. She wants him to become self-actualizing and no longer defensive and self-defeating. Thus, she clearly wants him to experience a new way of being in which he can grow and flourish and to see himself as capable of achieving that sort of change.

I have said that classical conditioning is only capable of sustaining permanent change, which the traditional behaviorist wants, if the client is capable of seeing the new desires instilled by reinforcement as in some respect better than the desires they are meant to defeat. As for operant conditioning, its ultimate success appears to rest on the capacity of the client for generalizing his new learning, and the possibility of generalizing is doubtful with the provision of external reinforcers alone. The cognitive behaviorist has an answer to these problems, and in her answer she recognizes two of the necessary aims of self-determination. In regard to the first problem, she can show the client that the new desires which counseling promotes are adaptive while the old desires are maladaptive. She can show him that there are good reasons for preferring the new desires. As for the second problem, she can acknowledge the possibility of internal reinforcers through the provision of positive role models, with whom the client can identify. By identifying with the perspective of the role model and perceiving the benefits accrued to her by behaving appropriately, the client acquires an essential skill for generalizing his behavior. Thus, the successful behaviorist is interested in cognitive advances in the client in perceiving himself from the role of the other (the therapist), and she wants him to see himself as a person capable of assuming this new prosocial perspective.

The rational counselors, while emphasizing the irrational rather than the maladaptive nature of the offender's beliefs, are similarly concerned with cognitive advances. They specifically want the offender to become more rational, responsible, and realistic as a consequence of counseling. To do so, they recognize that he must internalize the perspective of others so that he can at least more fully realize the consequences of his actions and thus be more able to cope with life's contingencies. They also want him to be able to perceive himself as a person capable of making this change to a more rational existence. That is, they want him to respect his own rational potential as much as they do.

SOME IMPLICATIONS

The preceding concludes my final arguments for the claim that self-determination is a goal of correctional counseling. It may be wondered what the philosophical or psychological implications of this claim may be. While I do not intend to fully explore such implications here, certain possibilities are suggestive. First, my claim seems to support the truth of a Rawlsian Liberalism or the idea that a just society is truly interested in equality of liberty and opportunity for all of its members, with liberty or self-determination taking precedence. While I argued previously that Libertarianism is not necessarily inconsistent with my views, the Rawlsian Liberals' interest in promoting the good for all members of society, and most especially those least well off, is more consistent with the justified state paternalism I endorse. Second, a particular normative claim can be assumed to follow from the truth of my descriptive claim about correctional counseling. That is, if a goal of correctional counseling is self-determination, then effective correctional counseling will be that which is likely to achieve it in the client. I have not presumed to rate the relative successfulness of any of the specific treatment modalities that have been discussed in terms of which is most likely to be effective. However, I think that insofar as any technique is guided by a clear understanding of what the development of self-determination requires, then counselors making use of it are more likely to be successful in meeting this goal with their clients. Third and last, my claim gives us reason to hope about our shared humanity. If some good can develop in even the worst offender we punish, it appears that much more good can develop in the rest of us.

NOTE

1. Gert, Culver, and Clouser, 1997, 104. This definition is slightly modified from their earlier definition. However, I believe it remains vulnerable to the same criticisms from Margolis.

Works Cited

Aboulafia, Mitchell. *The Mediating Self: Mead, Sartre, and Self-Determination.* New Haven, Conn.: Yale University Press, 1986.

Archard, David. "Self-Justifying Paternalism." *Journal of Value Inquiry*, 27, nos. 3-4 (December 1993): 341-352.

Aristotle. *Nicomachean Ethics,* 1144a-b, trans. Terence Irwin. Indianapolis, Ind.: Hackett, 1985.

Baker, Brenda. "Penance as a Model for Punishment." *Social Theory and Practice*, 18, no. 3 (Fall 1992): 311-331.

Beebe, Beatrice, Frank Lachmann, and Joseph Jaffe. "Mother–Infant Interaction Structures and Presymbolic Self- and Object Representations." *Psychoanalytic Dialogues*, 7, no. 2 (1997): 133-182.

Brace, Kerry. "Nonrelativist Ethical Standards for Goal Setting in Psychotherapy." *Ethics & Behavior*, 2, no. 1 (1992): 15-38.

Breggin, Peter R. *The Psychology of Freedom.* Buffalo, N. Y.: Prometheus Books, 1980.

Carney, Louis. *Corrections: Treatment and Philosophy.* Englewood Cliffs, N. J.: Prentice-Hall, 1980.

Clark, Michael. "The Sanctions of the Criminal Law." *Proceedings of the Aristotelian Society* (1997): 25-39.

Culver, Charles M. and Bernard Gert. *Philosophy in Medicine.* New York: Oxford University Press, 1982.

Deigh, John. "On the Right to be Punished: Some Doubts." *Ethics*, 94 (January 1984): 191-211.

Duff, R. A. *Trials and Punishments.* Cambridge, England: Cambridge University Press, 1986.

Dworkin, Gerald. "Paternalism." In *Paternalism*, ed. Rolf Sartorius. Minneapolis, Minn.: University of Minnesota Press, 1983, 19-34.

——. "Paternalism: Some Second Thoughts." In *Paternalism*, ed. Rolf Sartorius. Minneapolis, Minn.: University of Minnesota Press, 1983, 105-111.

——. "Paternalism." In *The Cambridge Dictionary of Philosophy*, ed. Robert Audi. Cambridge, England: Cambridge University Press, 1995, 564.

Feinberg, Joel. *Harmless Wrongdoing*. New York: Oxford University Press, 1988.

Foucault, Michel. *Discipline and Punish: The Birth of the Prison*, 2d ed., trans. Alan Sheridan. New York: Vintage Books, 1995.

Frankfurt, Harry. "Freedom of the Will and the Concept of a Person." In *Metaphysics*, ed. Ronald C. Hoy and L. Nathan Oaklander. Belmont, Calif.: Wadsworth, 1991, 367-376.

Gert, Bernard, Charles M. Culver, and K. Danner Clouser. *Bioethics: A Return to Fundamentals*. New York: Oxford University Press, 1997.

Greene, Roger L. *The MMPI: An Interpretive Manual*. Orlando, Fla.: Grune & Stratton, 1980.

Hampton, Jean. "The Moral Education Theory of Punishment." In *Punishment*, ed. A. John Simmons, Marshall Cohen, Joshua Cohen, and Charles R. Bietz. Princeton, N. J.: Princeton University Press, 1995. 112-142.

Hershey, Paul Turner. "A Definition for Paternalism." *The Journal of Medicine and Philosophy*, 10 (1985): 171-182.

Kohlberg, Lawrence. *Child Psychology and Childhood Education*. New York: Longman, 1987.

Kohlberg, Lawrence, Charles Levine, and Alexandra Hewer. *Moral Stages: A Current Formulation and Response to Critics*. New York: Karger, 1983.

Kratcoski, Peter C. *Correctional Counseling and Treatment*, 3d ed. Prospect Heights, Ill.: Waveland Press, 1994.

Kultgen, John. *Autonomy and Intervention: Parentalism in the Caring Life*. New York: Oxford University Press, 1995.

Lester, David and Michael Braswell. *Correctional Counseling*. Cincinnati, Ohio: Anderson Publishing Company, 1987.

Margolis, Joseph. "The Psychiatric Patient-Physician Relationship." In *The Clinical Encounter*, ed. Earl E. Shelp. Boston: Reidel, 1983, 173-186.

Merleau-Ponty, Maurice. *Phenomenology of Perception,* trans. by Colin Smith. New York: Humanities Press, 1962.

Menninger, Karl. "The Crime of Punishment." In *Contemporary Punishment*, Eds. Rudolph Gerber and Patrick McAnany. Notre Dame, Ind.: Notre Dame Press, 1972, 178-186.

Morris, Herbert. "A Paternalistic Theory of Punishment." *American Philosophical Quarterly*, 18, no. 4 (October 1981): 263-271.

Murphy, Jeffrie. "Marxism and Retribution." In *Punishment*, eds. A. John Simmons, Marshall Cohen, Joshua Cohen, and Charles R. Bietz. Princeton, N.J.: Princeton University Press, 1995, 3-29.

———. "Retributivism, Moral Education, and the Liberal State." *Criminal Justice Ethics*, 4, no. 1 (Winter/Spring 1985): 3-11.

Nozick, Robert. *Philosophical Explanations*. Cambridge, Mass.: The Belknap Press, 1981.

Patterson, Cecil. *Theories of Counseling and Psychotherapy*, 2d ed. New York: Harper & Row, 1973.

Pincoffs, Edmund. "Virtue, the Quality of Life, and Punishment." *Monist*, 63 (April 1980): 172-184.

Prust, Richard. "How to Treat a Criminal." *Public Affairs Quarterly*, 2 (July 1988): 33-50.

Quinn, Warren. "The Right to Threaten and the Right to Punish." In *Punishment*, ed. A. John Simmons, Marshall Cohen, Joshua Cohen, and Charles R. Bietz. Princeton, N.J.: Princeton University Press, 1995, 47-93.

Rawls, John. *A Theory of Justice*. Cambridge, Mass.: The Belknap Press, 1971.

———. "Two Concepts of Rules." *The Philosophical Review*, 64 (1955): 3-13.

Redmon, Robert B. "The Psychiatrist as Moral Advisor." *Theoretical Medicine*, 10, no. 4 (December 1989): 331-337.

Scoccia, Danny. "Paternalism and Respect for Autonomy." *Ethics*, 100, no. 2 (January 1990): 318-334.

Shafer-Landau, Russ. "Can Punishment Morally Educate?" *Journal of Value Inquiry*, 27, nos. 3-4 (December 1993): 341-352.

Slote, Michael. "Understanding Free Will." In *Metaphysics*, ed. Ronald C. Hoy and L. Nathan Oaklander. Belmont, Calif.: Wadsworth, 1991, 376-385.

Stratton, John G. "Correctional Workers: Counseling Con Men?" *Federal Probation*, 51 (June 1987): 24-27.

Tur, Richard. "Paternalism and the Criminal Law." *Journal of Applied Philosophy*, 2 (October 1985): 173-189.

Van Voorhis, Patricia, Michael Braswell, and David Lester. *Correctional Counseling and Rehabilitation*, 4th ed. Cincinnati, Ohio: Anderson Publishing Company, 2000.

Walker, Nigel. *Punishment, Danger and Stigma: The Morality of Criminal Justice*. Totowa, N. J.: Barnes & Noble Books, 1980.

Index

About the Author

Frances E. Gill was born in Raleigh, North Carolina and raised in Silver Spring, Maryland. She completed an undergraduate degree at St. Andrews Presbyterian College in Laurinburg, North Carolina, while majoring in both psychology and philosophy. After receiving a Master's degree in counseling at the University of Kansas, she was employed by the state of Kansas in the capacities of vocational rehabilitation counselor and correctional psychologist. She subsequently returned to graduate school at the University of Missouri where she received a Master's degree and a Doctoral degree in philosophy. Her chief philosophical interests include applied ethics, ethical theory, social and political philosophy, and ancient philosophy. She presently lives in High Point, North Carolina with her husband Eldon, son Daniel, and dogs Bricky and Lucky.